the WHOLE hog

Carol Wilson &
Christopher Trotter

PAVILION

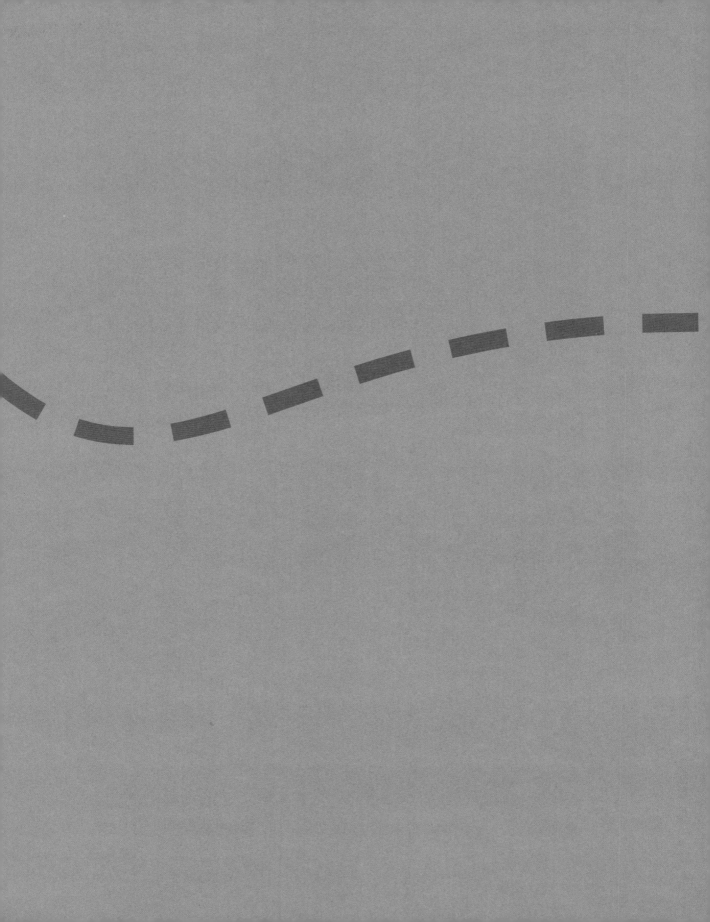

Contents

Introduction 009

The Cuts 020

Bacon and Ham 080

Sausages and Blood Puddings 142

Intriguing Others 212

Hog Roast 266

Index 276

the recipes

the cuts

Roast pork   38
    Roast rolled leg of pork with sesame
      potatoes and wild garlic apple sauce   39
    Honey roast pork with roast potatoes
      and apples   40
    Slow-roast shoulder of pork   42
    German roast pork   43
PERFECT CRACKLING   44
Pork and leek pie   47
Loin of pork with mustard
    and vermouth   48
Burmese golden pork   50
Hot and sour soup   52
Sweet and sour pork   54
Medallions of pork with orange   56
Pork fillet with caraway and tomatoes   57
Braised pork belly with fennel   59
Boiled pork belly with lentils   60
Cinghiale in dolce-forte   63
Hungarian goulash   64
Ragout of pork with prunes and leeks   66
Pork chops with chicory and lemon   67
Casserole of pork with fresh herbs and ale   68
Pork with plums   70
Pork with creamed leeks   72

Loin of pork with lemon
    and mushroom sauce   73
Baked chops in foil with apple and honey   75
Escalopes of pork with avocado and sage   76
Spare ribs   77
    Sauces: red pepper, sweet and sour,
    American   78

bacon

Steamed pork, bacon and leek pudding   94
Asturian bean stew   95
Spaghetti carbonara   96
Ragged Jack Kale with smoked bacon
    and Anster cheese   97
Leek and smoked bacon risotto   99
Salads   100
    Frisée and bacon   101
    Salad of bitter greens with poached
      eggs and prosciutto   102
    Salad with potato and mustard
      dressing   103
    Salsa verde   103
    Prosciutto with fruits   103

Dean & Deluca croque signor 104
BLT 105

ham

To cook a ham in comfort 126
Leek and ham with cheese sauce 127
Ham and haddie 128
Ham, chicken and mushroom pie 130
Feijoada 133
Tomato, ham and herb tarts 134
Ham with asparagus and Hollandaise 136
Pease pudding 137
Pea and ham soup 139
THE HAM SANDWICH 140

sausages

Making sausages 172
  Homemade sausages 174
  Homemade mash 176
  Other sausage mixes: Wiltshire,
    spicy sage, Italian 177
SAUSAGE SANDWICH 178
Sausage in brioche 181
Scotch eggs 182
Sausage rolls 184
Spanish stew with tripe and chickpeas 185
Tortilla con chorizo 187
Olla podrida 188
Meatballs in tomato sauce 191
Pounti 192
Choucroute 194
  Homemade choucroute 195
  Choucroute garni 196

Petit salé 197
Galician soup 198
Bigos 201
Fricadeller 202
Pâtés and terrines 204
  Country pâté 205
  Pork and pistachio terrine 206
  Pig(eon) terrine 209
  Rillettes 210
  Meat loaf 211

intriguing others

Bath chaps 234
Kidneys with mustard and mushrooms 236
Brawn 238
Faggots 241
THE BIG BREAKFAST 242
Pig's liver with lemon and honey 246
Cassoulet 248
  Cheat's cassoulet 249
  Traditional cassoulet 250
Castilian pig's trotters 253
Pied de cochon Ste Menéhould 255
Pork pie 256
Pork scratchings 258
Stock 259
Tomato sauce 260
Madeira sauce 261
Sauce gribiche 262
Pastry 263
Skirlie 263
Lardy cake 264
White bread 265

introduction

The pig, a most fascinating and iconic creature, has been both reviled and revered at various times throughout history. Often misrepresented as greedy, lazy and dirty, the pig has gradually achieved a more prominent and pleasing role in popular culture.

Round, jolly pigs are portrayed as loveable characters in nursery rhymes and children's literature, such as the tale of *The Three Little Pigs*, Beatrix Potter's *Little Pig Robinson* and *Pigling Bland*, and Alison Uttley's *Sam Pig*. Pigs appear in art and advertising and as ornaments and piggy banks. Despite their pleasingly round and piglike shape, it is widely believed that piggy banks were not named after the animal. In the Middle Ages, jars and containers were made of a clay called 'pygg'. People stored salt and saved coins in the jars, which themselves became known as 'pyggs'. By the eighteenth century, this clay was no longer used and the containers were made of ceramic, but retained the name 'pygg'. Nineteenth-century English potters produced the containers in the shape of a pig, which looked appealing, particularly to children. In the Netherlands and German-speaking countries, where the pig is a symbol of luck and good fortune, it is traditional to give piggy banks as gifts. In Germany, pigs made of marzipan are given as gifts at Christmas and New Year for good luck.

In Celtic culture, pigs were associated with the Otherworld (the Lord of the Otherworld was usually depicted with a pig over his shoulder) and the feasts of the dead, and symbolised abundance. Swineherds were believed to be magicians and in Irish folklore swineherds could cross from the Otherworld to this world and back again.

Pigs even have their own patron saint – St Anthony the Great (also referred to as 'The Abbot'), an Egyptian Christian in the second century AD, who

Pulling down acorns
to fatten pigs was once an
important part of animal
husbandry: it is depicted
in many medieval
manuscripts.

lived in the desert as an anchorite (recluse) for parts of his life. St Antony
is also the patron saint of swineherds and pig keepers, and in art is normally
portrayed with a pig nearby. His link with pigs is somewhat complicated.
Skin diseases of the time were sometimes treated with applications of
pork fat mixed with herbs (which reduced inflammation and itching)
and Antony is credited with healing such conditions, so he was portrayed
in art accompanied by a pig. People who saw the paintings took them at
face value and thought there was a direct connection between Antony and
pigs; thereafter, people who worked with swine took him as their patron.

The origin of the word 'pig' is unclear: the *Oxford English Dictionary*
suggests it is Middle English (the period between the Norman invasion and
about 1470). The word 'pork' refers to the edible flesh of a pig and is
derived from the French *porc* and Latin *porcus* words for 'pig'. 'Hog' is an
older English word, possibly of Celtic origin, for a domesticated pig.

THE DOMESTIC PIG

The pig is surely the most useful animal in the world. It was domesticated
from wild boar around 9000 years ago in the Near East. Written records
show that pigs were being reared in China around 5,000BC.

The ancient Egyptians farmed and ate pigs and regarded them as sacred
to the god Seth. The ancient Greeks also kept pigs and served pork at
feasts, but it was the ancient Romans who perfected the art of pig breeding,
rearing, cooking and curing the meat. Pork was so much in demand in
Rome that it had to be supplemented with imported supplies from Gaul,
where an abundance of wild pigs thrived in the forests.

Recent research by Durham University, England, has revealed that
domesticated pigs in Europe were introduced by Stone Age farmers from

the Middle East, while research from the Universities of Oxford and Durham has shown that the first European domestic pigs appeared in Central Europe and the areas we know as Italy and Germany around 1,500BC; by 800BC they had reached Britain.

The pig has had a major role in the economy wherever it is reared, although its consumption is prohibited by some religions: Jews, Muslims, Seventh Day Adventists and Rastafarians are all forbidden to eat pork on the grounds that the pig is unclean.

In fact, pigs are naturally clean, friendly, social and intelligent animals with a language that contains around 40 different expressions for communicating information. They can't tolerate heat, as they have no sweat glands, so they wallow in water or mud to cool down – this has given them their unfortunate reputation as 'dirty pigs'. Pigs are easy to keep and are very productive, with a gestation period of just four months. A sow produces an average of 10 piglets, although larger litters have been known. The young pigs grow at an incredible rate: in just six months piglets of 1.2 kg/2½ lb can increase their weight by an astonishing 5000 per cent.

In the past, many Europeans, whether country or town dweller, aspired to own at least one pig, which was regarded almost as a member of the family. Its health and condition were reported in letters to children living away from home and the loss of a pig was a terrible tragedy. In some areas pig clubs were formed, with members buying a part share of the pig. The funds were used to pay for the animal's upkeep, vet's bills, and so on. When the pig was killed, the meat was shared out amongst the members.

The pig has always been a most valuable animal. While it was alive, its dung could be used to enrich the soil, and after slaughter every part of the animal, from the tail to the trotters (except the squeak), could be utilised: the meat, offal, blood and fat for food; the bristles for brushes; the skin for shields, saddles, bags, shoes and modern-day dog chews and watch straps.

The bones were once made into gambling dice, tools and weapons, and today are used to manufacture gelatine and glue.

In France, mainly in the Périgord region, pigs are also valued for another reason. They are trained to hunt out highly prized (and expensive) truffles from underground. A trained pig can sniff out the unseen truffles from a distance of 6 metres/18 feet. Only female pigs are used since truffles have the same odour as male boar, and it's this musky aroma that attracts the sows.

The pig is an omnivore, which means that it is content to scavenge in and around a domestic smallholding eating household scraps and anything it finds, or to rootle around in woodland for acorns, hazelnuts, chestnuts, beechnuts, wild fruits and berries. Pigs have powerful snouts and sharp teeth, which allow them to dig mushrooms, tubers, roots and grubs from the ground. The pig's highly developed hearing, sense of smell and excellent sense of touch compensates for its poor eyesight.

In the Domesday Book, woodland was measured by the number of pigs it could support. English medieval swineherds were allowed 'pannage' – the right to graze their pigs on Royal forestland from Midsummer Day to 15 January, on condition that each pig had a ring through its nose. Pig ringing (which impeded foraging and deep rooting and minimised the damage to young trees) became law, with severe penalties for offenders. In the English county of Hampshire, pigs were turned out to forage in the New Forest, and the Hampshire hog was famous for the quality of its meat, which made excellent bacon and ham.

Nowadays, there are countless breeds of pig as a result of cross-breeding through the ages. Today, pigs are different from their ancestors, which were smaller, with longer snouts, a higher back, straight tails, longer bristles and more solid bones. Heavyweight pigs were (and still are) traditionally specially bred for charcuterie, bacon and ham.

Overleaf: Hams hanging in a row, ready for slices to be taken directly from them in Barcelona, Spain.

THE ANNUAL SLAUGHTER

Up until the twentieth century and the advent of refrigeration, it was traditional to slaughter pigs in the autumn and through winter, after they had been fattened all summer – they were not all killed at once, just a few at a time to ensure a constant supply of meat from autumn onwards. As much of the meat as possible was preserved by salting, drying or smoking to last until the following year. A whole or half pig could also be used as currency to pay the rent or a doctor's or grocer's bill.

The communal pig killing was a time for celebration, and in some European rural and mountain villages it remains a great social occasion. In Hungary, thousands flock to the country's biggest annual pig-killing festival in the village of Napkor near the Ukrainian border. In Spain the autumn pig killing is known as *la matanza* and in the Andalusia region of southern Spain fiestas celebrate the new supply of tasty morcillas (blood puddings), hams and sausages. An expression in rural France, *'Tout est bon dans le cochon!'* ('all of the pig – from head to tail– is good'), is associated with friends and family gathering to celebrate the killing of a pig.

Medieval illuminated manuscripts illustrate winter pig killings. An expert (usually a butcher) was called in to slaughter the pigs, and afterwards the blood was collected in a large tub and made into black puddings. Meanwhile, the pig was scalded and scraped, and the offal was removed, sorted and cleaned for immediate use, as it is not suitable for curing.

Once the slaughtered pig was cold, it was placed on a table and cut into the desired parts. The head, tail and trotters, which also cannot be cured, were cleaned and then boiled with onions, herbs, spices and vinegar until the meat fell off the bones. The meat was pounded to a paste, or chopped finely, before being turned into brawn with a tasty jelly made from the cooking liquid. It wouldn't keep long term, so had to be consumed within weeks.

The rest of the pig was cut up to be preserved in various ways to last throughout the long, bleak winter. The sides, shoulders and hams would be painstakingly rubbed with salt and placed in large barrels and tubs. The next day they were removed, cleaned and rubbed with salt again, then packed with more salt and placed under pressure, during which time brine formed to cure the meat and preserve it for many months. Some pieces were removed from the tubs after a few weeks and smoked, either in a smokehouse or hung in a domestic chimney.

Fresh pork was eaten only in the days after slaughter and cuts such as the roasted loin and leg were generally eaten only by the wealthy elite. Most people consumed preserved pork in its various forms.

The fat was cut into pieces and rendered down to use for frying. The remaining odds and ends and small bits and pieces of meat were finely chopped, stuffed into intestines, cured in salt and smoked to make sausages.

CHARCUTERIE

Pig meat, both fresh and cured, has long been used to create a staggering variety of products, including bacon, hams, pork pies, pâtés and terrines, confits, rillettes, sausages, salami and blood puddings. The art of charcuterie (from the French *chair cuite* – cooked meat) was originally a method of preserving meat.

It was widely practised in Ancient Rome, and the Roman expertise at curing meat spread throughout their Empire. The judicious and skilful use of salt, herbs and spices has produced a multitude of delicacies, particularly in Italy, Spain and France.

In fifteenth-century France, the *charcutiers* formed local guilds in each city. The members produced a range of cooked or salted and dried meats, which varied from region to region. The only raw meat the charcutiers were allowed to sell was unrendered lard.

A RICH CULINARY TRADITION

Pork remains a favourite meat in many European countries (including Denmark, where there are as many pigs as people), which has led to the creation of an extraordinary variety of dishes and a wealth of specialities using both fresh and cured pork. Europe has a rich culinary tradition of wonderfully tasty pork products: the spicy sausages and salamis of Germany, Poland, France, Italy and Spain; the blood puddings of France, Italy, Spain, Britain and Ireland; a huge choice of hams with an intense, lingering flavour and highly aromatic fat such as *jamón Ibérico*, Parma ham and Ardennes ham; and the quintessentially English raised pork pies, admired throughout the world, and one of the great triumphs of British cuisine.

THE CUTS

choosing pork

These days we can enjoy fresh pork all year round, and global demand is increasing steadily. However, it is important when buying pork to choose free-range, organic or rare breed meat.

Organic and free-range meat is from contented pigs, raised in the fresh air on a natural diet. There is growing interest in farming traditional breeds, which were once common but are now designated as rare. These pigs live outdoors and mature slowly without the need for growth promoters, hormones or antibiotics. The rising popularity of heritage breeds such as the British Lop, Berkshire, Gloucestershire Old Spot, Large Black, Middle White, Tamworth and Welsh is due to their meat, which is fine-grained, mouth-wateringly succulent and full of flavour, because the animals take longer to mature than breeds selected for intensive farming methods.

Huge changes in farming methods over the years have increasingly led to pigs being intensively reared in large sheds attached to a slaughterhouse. These unfortunate animals spend their lives indoors, in distressing conditions on slatted floors without straw, which completely goes against their natural instincts to root around for their food. They then pass along an assembly line to emerge as carcasses, but their meat has poor eating qualities, being very lean, dry and lacking in flavour. In some EU countries, pregnant sows are kept in farrowing pens without room to even turn around and are, in effect, just breeding machines, although this practice is illegal in Britain and will become illegal in the rest of Europe in 2013.

BUYING AND STORING PORK

Some producers inject pork products, such as chops and roasting joints, with water and additives 'to retain the moisture and improve eating quality'. As a consequence, the meat has an unpleasant 'woolly' texture when cooked and lacks flavour. It is, therefore, important to read the label if you buy meat in a supermarket, or to ask your butcher whether the meat you are buying is 100% pork.

When you buy pork, the flesh should be pink and fine-grained, with firm white fat. Joints, chops and steaks will keep for 2–3 days and large roasting joints up to four days, if refrigerated. Minced pork and offal should be eaten on the day you buy them.

Pork is suitable for home freezing. To lessen the chance of damage to its texture, freeze pork quickly and use frozen pork within six months. Thaw out, loosely wrapped, in the refrigerator and allow to come to room temperature before cooking.

Different cuts suit different cooking techniques and methods, as described for each cut in 'Identifying the cuts' overleaf. Whatever the cut, pork is never served pink or underdone.

IDENTIFYING THE CUTS

Different cuts of pork have various names, according to the country and, sometimes, even the region of their origin. It's not possible to include all the names and their regional variations, but from the point-of-view of the butcher, the pig is always divided into four main areas:

SHOULDER

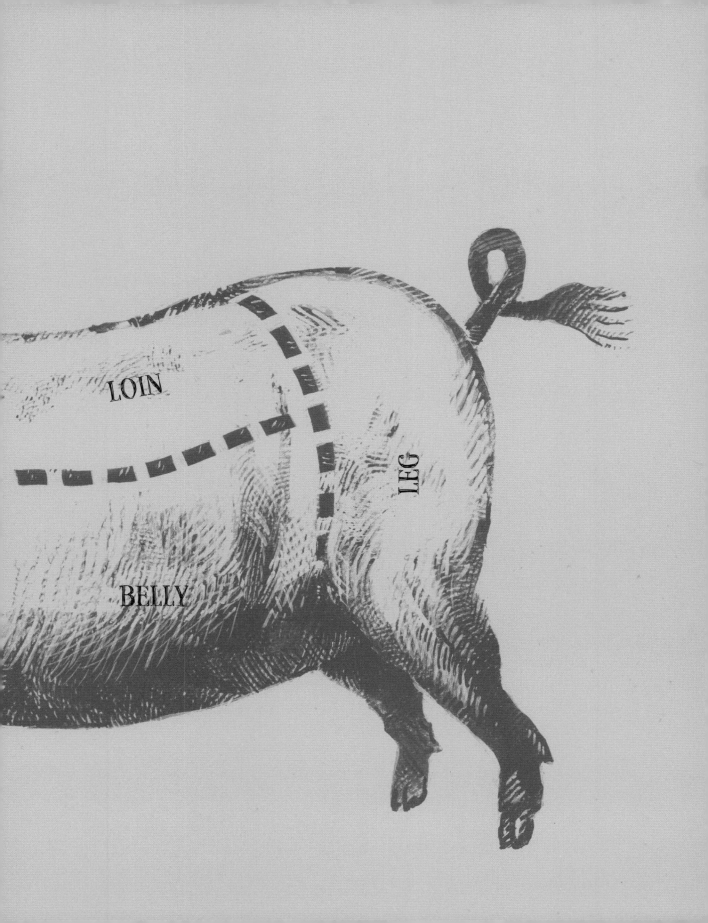

Belly comes from the underside of the pig and is fairly fatty. It may be sold as boneless slices or as a piece of pork belly, on or off the bone, which makes an inexpensive roasting joint. Rub the fat with salt and score with a sharp knife, then slow-roast the joint to produce wonderfully tender, succulent meat and crisp crackling. Joints can be boned, rolled and stuffed and belly slices can be grilled, fried or roasted. Pork belly is braised gently in China's famous 'red pork', and is cooked slowly with tomatoes, haricot beans (navy beans in the United States), spices and molasses in the classic American dish 'pork and beans'.

Blade is from the shoulder/top of the front leg and is usually roasted on the bone or cut into steaks or chops for braising. *Grillades* is the French name for thin blade steaks cut in a fan shape, which are usually grilled.

Cuts:
1. Blade
2. Chops
3. Belly

Chops come from the loin, chump (behind the loin) or spare rib and often include the kidney. They can be fried, grilled, casseroled or baked in the oven (see page 75). In Eastern Europe it is traditional to serve pork chops with sauerkraut (see page 194). In Spain *chuletas* refer to loin chops, while *costillas* can refer to either pork chops or spare ribs.

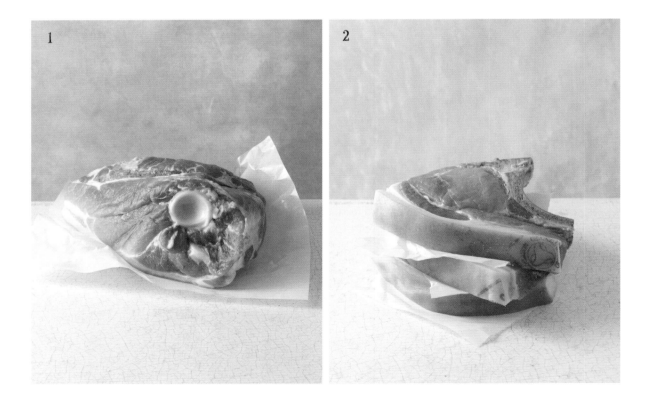

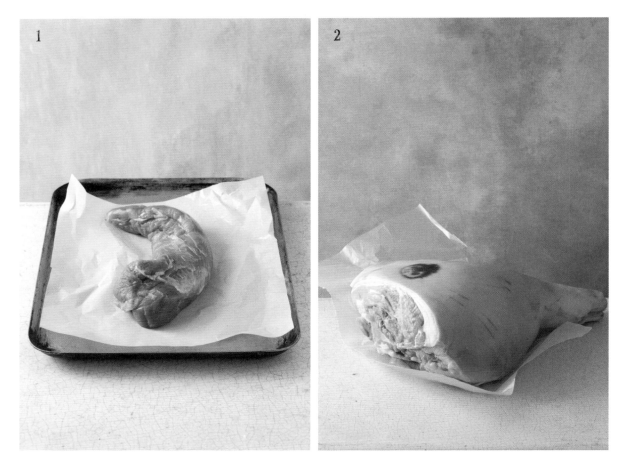

Cuts:
1. Fillet or tenderloin
2. Leg
3. Loin
4. Rack of pork 'frenched'

Diced pork is usually cut from the shoulder, is quite tough and is best used in slow-cooked stews and casseroles. If you want lean diced pork, ask for leg meat and cut it into the size you need. *Bosanski lonac* (Bosnian pot) is a traditional dish that has been enjoyed by rich and poor for generations; pork and various vegetables are layered in a deep pot, then covered with water, stock or wine. It was originally cooked in the fireplace or in a pit in the ground. *Ciorba* (sour soup) is a Rumanian speciality in which pieces of pork are simmered with onions and seasonings; a small glass of vinegar is added and the soup is thickened with soured cream.

Fillet or **tenderloin**, taken from the hind part of the loin, is lean and ideal for roasting or stuffing. Slices of pork fillet can be grilled, fried or casseroled. Smoked tenderloin such as the *poledwica* is a speciality of Eastern Europe.

Leg is lean and tender and is excellent for roasting, either on the bone or boned, rolled and stuffed. It can be roasted long and slow at a low heat, or fast at a higher heat. Leg steaks can be grilled or fried; they can be thinly sliced into strips or diced for stir-frying. A celebrated dish from Peru involves coating a boned and rolled leg of pork with a spicy mixture and

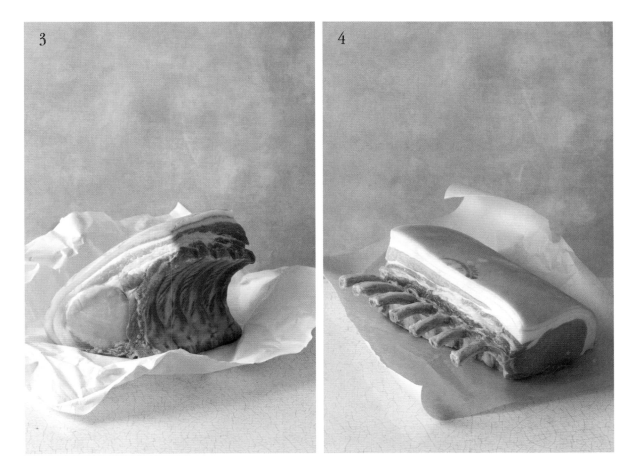

simmering in stock until tender. The pork is then browned in hot lard, sliced and served with rice or potatoes. Curiously, although it is always made with fresh pork, it is called *Jamón del País* (*jamón* being the Spanish word for ham).

Loin is a prime lean cut suitable for roasting and sometimes includes the kidney. It can be roasted on the bone or boned and stuffed, and cooked either long and slow, or fast at a higher heat. The skin can be scored with a sharp knife and becomes golden and crisp as it cooks. In Italy and Spain, a favourite way of cooking loin is slowly in the oven in milk: this produces delectably tender meat. In Spain the loin is called *lomo; lomo adobado* is a cured loin. *Kasseler rippchen* (roasted smoked pork loin) is a well-known German dish, which is believed to have originated in the German city of Kassel.

Rack of pork is a loin roast with the rib bones 'frenched' (trimmed of all extra meat). This cut is also used for crown roast of pork (two loins tied together to form a ring).

1

Cuts:
1. Spare ribs
2. Shoulder

Shoulder is quite fatty and can be roasted (bone in or boneless), braised or casseroled. If roasted, it is cooked long and slow at a low heat, resulting in meltingly tender and juicy meat. Boneless rolled shoulder of pork is succulent and flavoursome; it is tied into a joint of equal thickness so that it cooks evenly. Shoulder steak is best slowly braised. Smoked pork shoulder is often included in *bigos* (see page 153), Poland's ubiquitous sauerkraut stew.

Spare ribs can be cut into individual riblets and grilled or roasted. Smoked rib meat is the principal ingredient of *żurek*, a Polish rye-flour soup. Barbecued ribs are popular all over Europe, north America and parts of Asia, and are frequently marinated in a sweet/spicy mixture before cooking (see page 78). Spare rib chops are large and meaty and marbled with fat. They require longer, moister cooking than loin chops and make excellent casseroles.

Pork steaks are cut from the loin, leg or shoulder. Boneless, tender and juicy, they are best grilled, fried or barbecued.

2

WILD BOAR

The wild boar is the ancestor of the domestic pig. Large and fierce with its thick bristles and powerful tusks, the boar came to represent bravery and fearlessness across Europe. The image of a boar's head symbolised a courageous warrior who would fight to the death.

A boar's head was also a symbol of hospitality, dating back to the custom of serving boar's head at great feasts in the time of the Roman Empire. It later became a popular sign of inns and public houses. In medieval England, it was customary to serve a boar's head at Christmastide. The splendid Christmas feasts of the Middle Ages were extravagant events, according to the wealth of the host. (Note that the word 'banquet' didn't come into use until after the medieval period). Richard II's Yuletide feast was reputed to have catered for ten thousand people daily over the 12 days of Christmas. On Christmas Day, a boar's head glazed with aspic jelly and garlanded with herbs and leaves, and with its tusks gilded with gold leaf, was carried to the table accompanied by a fanfare of trumpets and the singing of a seasonal carol.

It was also customary to decorate the boar's head with lard piped in intricate patterns and the finely chopped jelly made from boiling the bones and meat trimmings.

Hunting wild boar was a popular pastime of the aristocracy all over Europe. In Britain, wild boar had become extinct by the end of the fourteenth century due to over-hunting. John of Gaunt (1340–1399), the fourth son of Edward III, is reputed to have killed the last wild boar in the country at Stye Bank in Yorkshire. Wild boars were reintroduced into England from the Continent, but by the seventeenth century had become extinct once again.

Wild boar still roam the forests of Italy and France, where they are hunted as game. In France, hunting (*la chasse*) is a favourite pastime and is considered to be a rite of passage. Wild boar (*sanglier*) has been the chief game animal and a major food source for more than a thousand years, and, is now a sought-after gastronomic speciality. The hunting season extends from September to January and is confined to Wednesday, Saturday and Sunday. The meat makes a hearty dish when cooked in wine and this traditional dish is known as *civet de sanglier*. Boar is also made into meatballs (*boules de Picolat*), dried sausage (*saucissons de sanglier*), pâté (*pâté de sanglier*) and air-dried hams.

Wild boar are a great irritation to fruit farmers. An adult boar will often stand on its hind legs against the trunk of a cherry tree and pull down the branches, causing them to break off, so that the young animals can enjoy the juicy fruits. They also love to eat the tender, new shoots on grape vines, and it's quite easy to spot the stunted growth on the vines bordering scrubland where the boars live.

It's a similar story in Italy, where hunters introduced Eastern European boar (*cinghiale*) to augment the native stock. Unfortunately, this proved to be a disaster for agriculture, with herds of boar roaming the countryside, including the many vineyards, for food. Hunting the marauding boar is a popular pastime in the autumn.

Spello, an ancient town in central Italy, celebrates the feast of Corpus Domini 60 days after Easter, with processions through the narrow streets, some of which are carpeted with thousands of flowers arranged in intricate patterns. Everyone later sits down to enjoy a meal, at which the main dish is *cinghiale in dolce-forte* – wild boar braised with pine nuts, raisins, chocolate, spices and prunes. The intriguing combination of chocolate, dried fruits, spices and red wine dates back four hundred years and produces a wonderfully flavoursome dish with a deep rich flavour (see page 62–63).

Nowadays, boar is farmed in many countries and is available all year round, although the flavour is not as strong as that of wild boar. Wild boar differ from domesticated pigs in a number of ways; they stand larger at the shoulder than at the haunch and their tails do not curl, but are straight. Unlike pork, wild boar is a red meat with a very tasty, slightly gamey flavour similar to venison, which becomes more pronounced as the animal ages. The flesh contains 70 per cent red fibres and 30 per cent white, compared to domestic pigs, which are 80 per cent white fibres and 20 per cent red. Boar meat is noted for its flavour and leanness and is sold either as fresh or frozen meat or processed into hams, pâtés, pies and sausages. Prized cuts are the saddle and haunches, which can also be smoked to produce wild boar ham. Other cuts include loin, shoulder, loin chops, leg steaks and fillet. The meat from male boars over the age of two years is very strong and is really only suitable for sausages.

The traditional way to cook wild boar is to marinate it in red wine, herbs and spices and then cook it slowly for several hours – a method that tenderises the rather dry, sometimes tough, flesh. Nowadays, it is more usual to use meat from younger animals with tender flesh, which cuts down on the cooking time. The flesh of young wild boar (up to the age of 16 months) is tender enough to fry or roast.

ACCOMPANIMENTS

Herbs that go well with pork include sage, rosemary and thyme. Sage is traditionally cooked with pork because it helps to digest the rich meat and is beneficial to digestion. The use of herbs, fruits and seasoning date back through history; Hannah Glasse, in her book *The Art of Cookery made Plain and Easy* (1747), gave a recipe for a sauce for roast pig: '...take a large piece of bread without the crust. Boil it in 1 pint of water with a little sugar, a few currants, a blade of mace and six peppercorns. Let it boil for about 5 minutes, remove the mace and peppercorns, drain off the water carefully. Beat up the bread to a thick sauce with a large lump of butter and a glass of red wine.'

Aromatic spices such as juniper, allspice and caraway also work well with pork. Strong-flavoured, warmly aromatic caraway is popular in pork dishes from Eastern and Central Europe and in Germany. The sweetly aromatic heat of paprika is the favourite flavouring for pork in southeast Europe, while smoked paprika is much used in Spanish and Mediterranean cookery. The French flavour their pork dishes with rosemary, juniper and garlic, while Italians prefer the aniseed flavour of fennel and sweetly mild marjoram as well as the more pungent garlic and juniper.

In North America, for example, cranberries, peaches, pineapple and apples are used in garnishes and sauces. South American cookery uses spicy ingredients such as cumin, cinnamon, cloves and hot peppers with pork, while Latin American pork dishes frequently incorporate chillies and sweet peppers plus sweet fruits, limes and corn.

Sauerkraut, or fermented cabbage, is a favourite accompaniment to roast pork in Germany, Eastern and Central Europe (as are fresh red or white cabbage and dumplings), and also in northern France, where it is known as *choucroute* (see page 194–5).

Asian cuisine combines pork with seafood: in Vietnam a popular dish is braised pork and steamed rice flavoured with fish sauce and shrimp paste; pork rolls with shrimps are a favourite dish in Taiwan; while shrimps and scallops are combined with minced pork to provide the filling for Chinese *shu mai*, a dim sum (steamed dumpling) speciality.

THE RECIPES

ROAST PORK

I think that, of all the roast meats, pork is my favourite since it's easier to get right than lamb or beef and it makes the best, most luscious gravy. There are so many accompaniments and herbs and seasonings that go well with roast pork and it can sit around for a while and not spoil. It is very important, to get the basics right, but from then on the world is your oyster!

A little note on fat: I am a firm believer that you need fat to cook a joint of meat and I would go so far as to say that animal fat in moderation is better for you than artificially prepared spreads and margarines. So, buy a piece of meat with a decent covering of fat and, if you don't want to eat it, trim it off AFTER cooking.

Here are several variations on roast pork, both on and off the bone. The first two recipes give the joint an initial blast at a high oven temperature, to ensure crisp crackling, then reduce the heat to give you succulent meat. Another way to ensure deliciously tender meat is to cook the pork joint for several hours at a very low temperature: there are two recipes to illustrate this technique.

A basic rule of thumb for the perfect roast is to leave the pork joint at room temperature for 1 hour before cooking. This takes the chill off the meat, and makes the cooking more even.

roast rolled leg of pork with sesame potatoes and wild garlic apple sauce

Wild garlic grows in woods and hedgerows from late April to May. Pick your own or look for it in farmers' markets. At other times of the year, you could add a garlic clove, lightly bruised, to the apples, and remove it before serving the sauce.

SERVES 4

1 rolled leg of pork, about 1 kg/2¼ lb, with the skin deeply scored (see page 44)

olive oil for roasting

1 kg/2¼ lb Maris Piper or small floury potatoes, peeled

1 tbsp sunflower oil

1 tbsp sesame seeds

2 Bramley apples

1 tbsp elderflower cordial or water

2 tsp brown sugar

10 leaves of wild garlic, shredded (optional, see above)

salt

Preheat the oven to 240°C/475°F/gas 9. Rub the pork skin all over with salt and some olive oil. Place on a rack in a roasting tin and roast for 20–30 minutes until the skin is beginning to 'crackle' but not brown too much. Reduce the oven temperature to 190°C/375°F/gas 5 and roast for a further 30–40 minutes, allowing approximately 30 minutes per 500 g/1 lb 2 oz of meat. Leave to rest in a warm place for 15 minutes.

Meanwhile, toss the potatoes in the sunflower oil and put into a hot roasting tin. Roast in the oven alongside the pork until brown. After 50 minutes, sprinkle with sesame seeds and return to the oven until the seeds are just brown. Be careful not to allow the seeds to burn.

Peel and core the apples, cut into chunks and cook in a saucepan with the elderflower cordial (or water) and the brown sugar. Cook until just soft and beginning to break up. When cooked, take off the heat and mix in the wild garlic leaves.

Serve the pork with the apple sauce, sesame potatoes and a bright green vegetable, such as cabbage or spinach.

honey pork with roast potatoes and apples

This shows how the basic roasting method can be adapted to create a one-pot dish. From this recipe, you can go on and create your own versions – try using parsnips, butternut squash, red onions cut into wedges, rosemary, thyme . . .

SERVES 6

1 piece of pork loin on the
  bone, with 4–5 ribs, and
  the skin deeply scored
2 tbsp sunflower oil
50 g/2 oz butter
700 g/1½ lb Belle de
  Fontenay or other
  waxy potatoes such
  as Charlotte, scrubbed
8 shallots or little onions,
  peeled
2 Discovery apples or other
  sharp eating apple
1 tbsp clover honey
1 tsp wholegrain mustard
fresh sage leaves
2 tsp plain flour (optional)
250 ml/9 fl oz Heather Ale
  or other fragrant ale
salt and pepper

If you like, you can remove the bones and tie the meat back onto the bones for cooking.

Preheat the oven to 240°C/475°F/gas 9. Rub the pork skin all over with salt and a little oil. Place the meat in a roasting tin and roast for about 30 minutes, or until the crackling is beginning to form.

Remove the tin from the oven, pour in the oil and butter and add the potatoes and shallots. Cook for another 15 minutes, then reduce the heat to 190°C/375°C/gas 5 and cook for a further 30 minutes. Meanwhile, core the apples and cut into quarters. Combine the honey with the mustard.

Remove the tin from the oven and lightly brush the meat with the honey mixture, avoiding the crackling or it will soften. Add the apples and a few sage leaves to the vegetables, season and mix around, then put back into the oven for another 20 minutes, until everything is cooked. Remove the pork, cover lightly with foil and keep it warm in a low oven. Keep the vegetables warm in a separate dish.

To make the gravy, place the roasting tin on the hob and allow the juices to simmer. If you want a thicker gravy, sprinkle in the flour and stir in well, allowing it to colour a little. Add the ale and stir to combine. Strain into a pan and allow to simmer until a good pouring consistency – add water if necessary. Season and serve with the pork and vegetables.

slow-roast shoulder of pork

The shoulder is ideal for long, slow cooking since it has a good covering of fat. It's ideal as a lazy Sunday lunch dish because all the work is done the night before. Try to buy a small whole shoulder, which may mean finding a rare breed; however, if you can find only a large shoulder, which can weigh 6–7 kg/13–15 lb, then just buy part of it. Ask your butcher for a piece on the bone, as this helps to hold the shape and prevents it drying out during the long cooking time.

SERVES 8–10

1 shoulder of pork, about
  3 kg/6½ lb
12 garlic cloves, peeled
3–4 tbsp fennel seeds
4 or 5 dried red chillies
the juice of 6 lemons
4 tbsp olive oil
sea salt and freshly ground
  black pepper

Preheat the oven to 230°C/450°F/gas 8. Make slashes all the way down the skin of the pork about 1 cm/½ inch apart – I use a Stanley knife that I keep for this purpose since you can set the blade to 1 cm/½ inch depth and it won't go any deeper. Start at the top of the joint and score down as far as you can, then turn the meat around so you can complete the slash right down to the bottom edge.

Put the garlic and fennel seeds into a pestle and mortar and crush to a paste, then add the chillies and crush lightly. Mix in salt and pepper to taste. Rub this mixture all over the slashed skin of the shoulder, then put the pork on a rack in a roasting tin and roast for about 30 minutes. This should be enough time to blister the skin, which should start to go brown.

Remove the meat from the oven. Mix half the lemon juice with half the olive oil and pour all over the meat. Reduce the heat to 140°C/275°F/gas 1, return the meat to the oven and leave either overnight or all day, but certainly for at least 8 hours. Turn the meat occasionally and baste with the juices. The meat is ready when it falls off the bone or is soft under the skin, which should be crisp.

To complete the dish, remove the roasting tin from the oven. Transfer the pork to a carving board, lightly cover and leave to rest for about 30 minutes. Add the remaining lemon juice and olive oil to the roasting tin, whisking it until smooth. Cut slices of meat from different parts of the shoulder and serve with the sauce poured over.

German roast pork

There is a simplicity about this recipe that suggests it calls for pork of high quality, and, with a good covering of fat. You are getting the true essence of the meat, so unless you have a good piece from a rare breed or free-range animal don't try it. Ask your butcher to remove the skin, but keep it to make scratchings (see page 258).

SERVES 6

1 piece of pork loin on
  the bone with 4–5 ribs
  (get your butcher to half
  cut through the backbone
  between each rib and
  remove the skin)
8 rashers of streaky bacon
40 g/1½ oz butter
40 g/1½ oz plain flour
500 ml/18 fl oz pork stock
  (see page 259) or chicken
  stock
black pepper

Preheat the oven to 140°C/275°F/gas 1.

Season the pork with pepper and place in a roasting tin – fat side up. Place the bacon rashers over the roast so it is completely covered by bacon. Roast in the oven until it reaches 70°C/160°F on a meat thermometer – approximately 2½–3½ hours.

Remove the bacon and brown the pork under a hot grill, then leave to rest for at least 20 minutes.

Meanwhile, make the gravy. Make a beurre manié (see page 274) with the butter and flour. Chop up the cooked bacon and return it to the roasting tin. Place the tin over a high heat to brown the bacon, then pour in the stock and simmer for 5–10 minutes. Thicken the gravy by whisking in the beurre manié, a piece at a time. Strain into a jug or a gravy boat. Cut slices of pork through the half cut ribs and serve with the sauce.

PERFECT CRACKLING

Roast pork is a magnificent dish and perhaps one of the grandest of simple ways to cook pork. Crackling is well-loved and rarely manages to stay on the serving plate for more than a few moments at the beginning of a Sunday lunch; the crisp browned outer layer of crackling holding moist flavoursome meat within is irresistable.

How to get the best crackling

One way of getting good crackling is to score the fat at 3 mm/¼ inch intervals, running with the grain – ask your butcher if you prefer – I use a Stanley knife at home. Cook as you would for a normal roast.

Another way of cooking crackling is to cook your meat initially at 190°C/375°F/gas 5, then remove the pork from the roasting dish and use the juices for gravy. Next, turn the oven up to 230°C/450°F/gas 8 and remove the outer layer of fat from your piece of pork and return the fat to the hot oven. The meat remains moist and has time to stand before carving, and the crackling is crisp and hot. You must not baste the fat, as this will cause it to go hard and leathery.

A chef I worked with in Switzerland always swore by brushing the scored meat with wine vinegar the night before you cook it, as this will dry out the skin, thus allowing the skin to crisp up even more! But you have to remember to leave it overnight.

Pig ears

You can get delicious crunchy pig ears if you have them left over from cooking them on the pigs head for brawn (page 238). Press them between two plates and chill, then slice very thinly and fry in oil until crisp.

pork and leek pie

This is made rather like a 'blanquette', in that the meat is cooked first in a stock and then a sauce is made from the stock. In this recipe I have added leeks since the colour and flavour go so well with pork, but you can add whatever you like. You can also serve it without the pastry lid, or add some chopped fresh herbs. Parsley works well.

SERVES 6

1 kg/2¼ lb diced leg
  of pork
1 small onion, studded
  with 8 cloves
10 peppercorns
1 sprig of thyme
parsley stalks
2–3 large leeks, trimmed
60 g/2½ oz butter
50 g/2 oz plain flour,
  plus extra for dusting
1 tsp English or Dijon
  mustard
450 g/1 lb puff pastry
1 small egg, beaten,
  to glaze
salt and pepper

Place the meat in a pan with a lid and just cover with cold water. Bring to the boil and skim off the froth. Lower the heat to a gentle simmer and add the onion, peppercorns and herbs. Cover and simmer for about 1 hour or until the meat is just tender.

Slice the leeks, bring a pan of water to the boil and blanch the leeks for about 2 minutes, then drain and refresh them in cold water. Drain thoroughly and set aside.

Strain the stock from the meat and remove the herbs and onion. In another pan, melt the butter, then stir in the flour and cook for a few minutes (to form a roux), then slowly pour in about 500 ml/18 fl oz of the stock from the meat to form a sauce. Simmer for 15 minutes to reduce slightly, then add the mustard and check the seasoning. Add the cooked pork and the blanched leeks to the sauce and mix through. Allow to cool.

Place the mixture in a 1.5 litre/2½ pint pie dish. Roll out the pastry on a lightly floured surface to fit the dish. Brush the edges of the pie dish with a little beaten egg, then place the pastry on top, press down the edges firmly, flute the edges, and brush again with the egg. Decorate with pastry leaves and brush these lightly with egg. Allow to rest for 30 minutes before cooking. Preheat the oven to 230°C/450°F/gas 8.

Place the pie in the oven for 20 minutes until the pastry has set, then reduce the oven temperature to 180°C/350°F/gas 4 and cook for another 40 minutes.

loin of pork with mustard and vermouth

When we got married, my wife and I spent part of our honeymoon at Sharrow Bay Hotel in the Lake District, which in those days was owned by Francis Coulson and Brian Sack, the first people to run a true 'country house hotel'. It was certainly one of the best at the time. We returned a year later for our anniversary and got into a conversation with an American couple, Ann and Dick Baker. When they discovered it was our first anniversary, unbeknownst to us, they went and told the owners — who promptly arrived with cake and champagne! Ann was a keen cook and sent me an inspiring little book with a series of recipes put together by the 'Junior League of Palo Alto', of which she was a member. This recipe was for veal, but I adapted it to pork and it was very successful. Ask the butcher for the bones, which you can use to make the stock (see page 259), and the skin for pork scratchings (see page 258).

SERVES 6–8

2 kg/4½ lb piece of pork
  loin off the bone
75 g/3 oz butter
75 g/3 oz Dijon mustard
250 ml/9 fl oz pork stock
  (see page 259)
6 tbsp dry vermouth
100 ml/3½ fl oz double
  cream
4 tbsp chopped fresh parsley
salt and pepper

Preheat the oven to 150°C/300°F/gas 2.

Using a very sharp knife, trim most of the fat from the loin, leaving a very thin layer (keep the fat for a pâté or terrine – see page 205–9). Melt the butter and mix it with the mustard; spread the mixture all over the pork, with some salt and pepper. Put into a roasting tin and cook in the oven for 15 minutes, then pour the stock and vermouth over the meat and cook for a further 2–2½ hours, basting from time to time.

Remove the meat from the tin, cover loosely with foil and leave to rest for at least 10 minutes. Tilt the tin and spoon off as much of the fat as you can. Place the roasting tin on the hob and allow the juices to simmer, adding more stock if the sauce is a little too thick. Stir in the cream and a little splash more vermouth, then strain. Slice the pork and serve with the sauce and lots of chopped parsley.

Burmese golden pork

I include this Burmese recipe partly because my father was in Burma in the late 1940s, but it is not a cuisine I know much about. It's a dish that is supposed to keep for months in an enclosed jar. I have never tried this — perhaps one may prefer not to risk it nowadays!

SERVES 4–6

1 large onion, peeled
  and chopped
1 head of garlic, cloves
  peeled and crushed
100 g/3½ oz fresh root
  ginger, peeled and
  chopped
1 kg/2¼ lb lean pork
  (leg or loin), cut into
  2.5 cm/1 inch cubes
1 tsp salt
1 tbsp white wine vinegar
1 tsp chilli powder
100 ml/3½ fl oz
  groundnut oil
2 tsp sesame oil
1 tsp turmeric

Grind together in a processor or pestle and mortar the onion, garlic and ginger. Press the resulting mixture through a sieve or fine muslin cloth to extract the juice, and keep the residue.

Pour the liquid into a pan and add the pork, salt, vinegar and chilli powder and half the groundnut oil. Bring to a gentle simmer and cook for 1½ hours.

Heat the remaining groundnut oil with the sesame oil in another large, heavy-based pan until hot, then add the residue of the onion, garlic and ginger, stir in the turmeric and cook over a low heat for about 10 minutes; if it gets too dry add a little water.

Take half the cooked pork and mince it, then add it to the onion, garlic, ginger and turmeric mixture. Add this to the rest of the pork, stir everything together and continue cooking until the mixture is golden brown – this may take another 20 minutes. Serve with rice.

hot and sour soup

As with so many popular Chinese dishes, there are many different recipes from different regions. This one is probably more Beijing than Sichuan, as it is not spicy-hot with chillies. If you can't get fresh cloud ear mushrooms, the dried variety is fine, as here. If you can't get tiger lily buds, just use some extra mushrooms.

SERVES 4

30 g/1¼ oz dried small cloud ear
  mushrooms
5 dried Chinese mushrooms
  (shiitake, or flower mushrooms)
15 g/½ oz dried tiger lily buds
  (golden needles)
1 tbsp groundnut oil
2 garlic cloves, peeled and crushed
115 g/4 oz lean pork, shredded
1 litre/1¾ pints pork stock (see page 259)
  or chicken stock

5 spring onions – 3 chopped in 1 cm/
  ½ inch lengths and 2 chopped for garnish
50 g/2 oz bamboo shoots (canned are fine)
90 ml/3 fl oz Chinese black rice vinegar
  or red wine vinegar
2 tsp sugar
3 tbsp light soy sauce
2 tbsp cornflour
1 egg, beaten
115 g/4 oz firm bean curd, diced
1 tbsp sesame oil
ground white pepper

Put the dried mushrooms in separate bowls, add boiling water to cover
by about 5 cm/2 inch and leave to soak for 20 minutes. Put the tiger lily
buds in a small bowl and soak in warm water for 20 minutes. Drain and
slice the mushrooms. Drain the tiger lily buds and cut into 5 cm/2 inch
sections. Set aside.

Heat the groundnut oil in a large pot, then add the garlic and cook gently
for a couple of minutes. Add the pork and cook for a further 2 minutes.
Add the stock, mushrooms, tiger lily buds, spring onion lengths, bamboo
shoots, vinegar, sugar, soy sauce and white pepper to taste and bring to
the boil. Slake the cornflour with a little water and whisk into the soup
to thicken it, then simmer for 10–15 minutes.

To serve, stir in the beaten egg and reduce the heat, then add the bean
curd and simmer for 1 minute to warm through. Serve in hot bowls with
a drizzle of sesame oil on top and a sprinkling of chopped spring onions.

sweet and sour pork

This was probably my earliest initiation into Eastern food. My mother used to make a dish called sweet and sour pork and I believe it came from one of the late, great Robert Carrier's books. I remember thinking how exotic it was with the spicy flavours. My favourite part was the water chestnuts, which added a delicious crunch. Try to use light soy sauce, otherwise the dish will look brown.

SERVES 4

675 g/1 lb 7oz lean pork, cut into strips
1 tsp each sugar and salt
1 tsp light soy sauce
1 egg, lightly beaten
cornflour for coating
sunflower oil for shallow-frying
1 onion, peeled and sliced
2.5 cm/1 inch piece of fresh root ginger, peeled and sliced
2 red peppers, quartered, deseeded and sliced
2 garlic cloves, peeled and crushed

FOR THE SAUCE

1^1/4 tsp cornflour
100 ml/3^1/2 fl oz wine vinegar or rice vinegar
100 g/3^1/2 oz brown sugar
1 tbsp rice wine or pale dry sherry
4 tbsp light soy sauce
1 tbsp tomato purée (optional)

Mix the pork with the sugar, salt and soy sauce and leave to marinate for a few minutes, then add the beaten egg and mix. Roll the pork pieces in the cornflour and leave aside until the meat has started to exude moisture.

In a large pan, heat enough sunflower oil to shallow-fry the pork. Add the pork in batches and cook until each piece is light brown, then return all the pieces to the hot pan and cook for a few minutes until the pork is cooked through. Drain on kitchen paper and keep warm. Keep the pan with the oil on one side.

For the sauce, mix the cornflour with enough water to make a thin paste. Put the vinegar, sugar, sherry and soy sauce in a large pan and bring to the boil. Stir in the cornflour paste and keep stirring until the mixture thickens. Add the tomato purée, if using, and keep warm.

Pour off most of the oil from the first frying pan and, over a gentle heat, stir in the onion, ginger and peppers and cook until soft, then stir in the garlic and cook gently for a few more minutes. Add these to the sauce along with the pork and stir all together. Serve with rice.

medallions of pork with orange

Orange goes well with pork; I also love fruity sauces with ham. This idea comes from friends in America.

SERVES 4

2 x 250 g/9 oz pork fillets
1 tsp dry mustard
2 tbsp butter
2 tsp groundnut oil
125 ml/4 fl oz dry vermouth
125 ml/4 fl oz dry white
  wine
2 garlic cloves, peeled
  and crushed
225 ml/8 fl oz orange juice
grated zest of 1 orange
chopped fresh flat leaf
  parsley
salt and pepper

Cut the fillets into 2 cm/¾ inch thick slices. Combine the mustard with salt and pepper and rub into the meat.

Heat a large, heavy-based pan, add half the butter with a touch of groundnut oil and brown the meat on both sides on a high heat for a couple of minutes. Reduce the heat and cook for another 5 minutes. Pour in the vermouth and allow to bubble up, then remove the meat and keep warm.

Increase the heat, add the wine, garlic, orange juice and zest to the pan and reduce to about 3–4 tbsp. Take the pan off the heat and swirl in the remaining butter and the parsley. Return the pork to the pan and heat through, but don't boil again. Serve with tagliatelle or steamed rice.

pork fillet with caraway and tomatoes

This is a hybrid idea based on an American recipe, with the addition of tomato. I like the colours, and the flavour of caraway goes very well with the pork.

SERVES 4

2 x 250 g/9 oz pork fillets
seasoned flour
1 tbsp groundnut oil
100 g/3½ oz button
  mushrooms, sliced
1 tsp caraway seeds
300 ml/½ pint hot pork
  stock (see page 259)
4 ripe tomatoes, blanched,
  peeled, deseeded and
  quartered
4 tbsp double cream
salt and pepper

Cut the pork fillets into thin slices across the grain. Toss lightly in the seasoned flour, then shake off any excess flour.

Heat the oil in a wide sauté pan and quickly colour the meat on both sides. (You may have to do this in batches to avoid overcrowding the pan, in which case you will need to use a little more oil to prevent sticking.) Remove and set aside. Toss in the mushrooms and cook to lightly colour, then stir in the caraway seeds and return the meat to the pan. Add the hot stock. Reduce the heat and allow to simmer for 10–15 minutes until the pork is cooked through.

Add the tomatoes and cream and heat through but don't allow it to boil, or the cream will curdle. Check for seasoning and serve with rice or noodles.

braised pork belly with fennel

Fennel is a vegetable that goes well with pork and I use it often; the aniseedy flavour somehow cleans up the slightly cloying texture of the cheaper cuts. This recipe is very easy and really packs a punch of flavours, using not only fennel but also the wonderful French aniseed liquor or spirit pastis, which is flavoured with star anise. Pastis is a generic term, like whisky or gin, and there are several brands, such as Ricard or Pastis 51. Then, finally, there are fennel seeds, not to mention lots of garlic.

SERVES 4–6

1.5 kg/3 lb 5oz pork belly
2 tbsp vegetable oil
100 ml/3½ fl oz dry white wine
1 tbsp pastis
2 fennel bulbs, cut into quarters
10 ripe tomatoes, cut into quarters (with the cores taken out if that sort of thing concerns you)
12 garlic cloves, peeled and crushed
3 bay leaves
2 juniper berries
1 sprig of rosemary
2 tsp fennel seeds
the peel and juice of 1 lemon
salt and pepper

Preheat the oven to 150°C/300°F/gas 2.

Score the skin of the pork belly with a Stanley knife, then rub in salt and pepper. Heat a large ovenproof pan over a medium heat until hot.

Pour the vegetable oil into the pan and place the pork in, taking care as it will spit. Brown the meat all over, which will take a few minutes, then remove from the pan and set aside. Reduce the heat a little and if there is a lot of fat carefully drain some off. Pour in the wine and pastis and, using a wooden spoon, scrape up the bits left by the browning pork.

Return the pork to the pan with the skin facing up and strew the vegetables and garlic around it along with the herbs, then sprinkle the fennel seeds all over. Lastly, pour in the lemon juice and add the lemon peel. Cover with a lid or foil and cook in the oven for 2 hours, turning the meat over and basting halfway through.

Serve in slices, on the bones if you like (but this may make the slices quite thick), with spoonfuls of the intensely flavoured vegetables and juices. Fabulous with mash.

boiled pork belly with lentils

A great celebratory dish, created by Fergus Henderson. The pork belly needs to be cured first, which helps to set the fat — the fat is an important part of this dish. So cure it for at least 5 days and up to 10 days in the pickling liquid, then cook it and serve the meltingly tender pork with the Puy lentils. You will need a very large pot to cook the pork.

SERVES 8

2 kg/4½ lb piece of pork belly,
  with the skin and bone still on,
  brined (see page 234)
2 whole carrots, peeled
2 onions, peeled and stuck
  with 5 cloves each
2 sticks of celery
1 head of garlic, cloves peeled
  and left whole
fresh parsley stalks, sage and thyme
1 tsp crushed black
  peppercorns

FOR THE LENTILS
400 g/14 oz Puy lentils
1 tbsp olive oil
1 onion, peeled and finely chopped
1 leek, trimmed, finely diced and washed
1 carrot, peeled and finely diced
4 garlic cloves, peeled and crushed
stock from cooking ham or water
1 tsp chopped fresh parsley
3 fresh sage leaves, chopped
salt and pepper

Take the pork belly (brined) and rinse well. Place in a large pot, cover with water and slowly bring to just to the boil. Skim off any froth or scum, then taste the liquid. If it is very salty, discard and bring the pork to the boil again in fresh water. Lower the heat and add the other ingredients for the pork. Simmer very gently for about 2½–3 hours. It should be soft but not disintegrating.

Rinse the lentils and put into a pan with cold water to come about 3 cm/1 inch above them. Bring to the boil, then simmer for 15 minutes. Drain in a sieve and set aside.

Heat the olive oil in another larger pan, then sweat the onion, leek and carrot until softened but not coloured. Add the garlic and stir for a few moments, then add the lentils and enough stock or water to just cover the lentils and simmer for 5–10 minutes. Add the parsley and sage and season with salt and pepper. The lentils should be softening but not a mush. Serve with the pork.

SERVES 6

1.5 kg/3 lb 5 oz wild boar, cut into
  3 cm/1¼ inch cubes
3 tbsp olive oil
1 onion, peeled and finely chopped
50 g/2 oz bitter chocolate
1 tbsp pine nuts
75 g/3 oz prunes, stoned and halved
½ tsp ground chilli
grated zest of 1 orange
1 tbsp raisins
1 tbsp brown sugar
salt and pepper

FOR THE MARINADE

500 ml/18 fl oz red wine
100 ml/3½ fl oz red wine vinegar
1 bay leaf
1 sprig of fresh thyme
1 tsp each ground
  cinnamon and allspice
½ tsp freshly grated
  nutmeg
1 carrot, peeled and chopped
1 onion, peeled and chopped
1 stick of celery, chopped

Place all the marinade ingredients in a saucepan and bring to the boil, then leave to cool – this takes quite a long time, but the marinade must be cold before you add the meat. Put the meat into a bowl, cover with the marinade and leave for 2 days.

Strain the marinade into a bowl, reserving the meat and discarding the vegetables. Pat the meat dry with absorbent kitchen paper. Heat the olive oil in a pan, add the onion and cook for a few minutes. Add the meat and brown lightly, then add the rest of the ingredients, along with the strained marinade. Bring to the boil and skim, then simmer very gently until the meat is cooked, about 2 hours. Check for seasoning and serve with polenta.

cinghiale in dolce-forte

I have not included any recipes specifically for wild boar, as the breed has been domesticated in the United Kingdom and most pork recipes can be used interchangeably. When I worked in Switzerland, we did get the occasional *sanglier*, or wild boar, brought into the kitchen during the hunting season (*La Chasse*). This recipe, which Carol found and I have played with, is so intriguing because of its use of chocolate and spices. Farmed wild boar does not, strictly speaking, need to be marinated – but the marinade adds great flavour, although you will need to start two days in advance.

Hungarian goulash

I can remember the first time I cooked this dish – I'd never used paprika in such quantity before. It was also the first time I'd drunk Bull's Blood, the rich, deep-red wine from Hungary, so I have hazy memories of eating goulash in my cold, tiny bedsit in London and drinking far too much strong, red wine. The recipe I used then came from a book called *One-pot Cooking*, or something like that, sadly now long since lost due to disintegration from overuse. However, here is a more authentic recipe. It is somewhat like a soup, with the liquid adding to the juiciness of the meat.

SERVES 4

3 tbsp lard or vegetable oil
1 large onion, peeled and
  chopped
3 garlic cloves, peeled
  and pulped
2 tbsp hot paprika
1/2 tsp caraway seeds
1/2 tsp ground cayenne
  pepper
900 g/2 lb pork shoulder,
  cut in 2.5 cm/1 inch dice

2 large ripe tomatoes,
  blanched, peeled and
  chopped (or you can
  use 200 g/7 oz canned
  chopped tomatoes)
1 large red pepper,
  deseeded and chopped
2 large potatoes, peeled
  and cut into small dice
salt and pepper

Heat the lard or vegetable oil in a large casserole until hot. Cook the onion until soft but not brown, then reduce the heat and add the garlic, paprika, caraway seeds and cayenne pepper. Stir for about 5 minutes. Add the pork and raise the heat, stirring to coat the meat in the mixture, then cook until lightly browned. Pour in warm water to just cover the meat and bring to a simmer. Cover and cook gently for 1 hour, or until the pork is tender.

Remove the lid, stir in the tomatoes and red pepper and simmer, uncovered, for 30 minutes.

Add the potatoes and cook until they are just done but not breaking up. Season and serve.

ragout of pork with prunes and leeks

This could be seen as a variation of the traditional Scottish dish Cock-a-leekie, in which a whole chicken is cooked in a broth with leeks and then prunes are added to sweeten it.

SERVES 4

12 prunes
200 ml/7 fl oz medium
  cider
2 x 250 g/9 oz pork fillets
4 tbsp flour seasoned with
  salt and pepper
4 tbsp olive oil
2 medium leeks, trimmed
200 ml/7 fl oz double
  cream
1 tsp chopped fresh thyme
salt and pepper

If using dried prunes, you need to start this the night before. Put the prunes into a bowl, add the cider and leave to soften overnight. Ready-to-eat prunes need to be soaked only for 1–2 hours.

Cut the fillets into 2 cm/¾ inch pieces across the grain. Dry the pork with absorbent kitchen paper, then toss it in the seasoned flour and shake off any excess flour. Heat half the olive oil in a frying pan. Brown the meat in the pan on a high heat to colour both sides. Make sure the pan is not crowded – cook in batches if necessary. Once all the meat has browned, return it to the pan, reduce the heat and cook for 5 minutes.

Slice the leeks across the grain into thin rounds. Remove the meat from the pan and add the leeks, adding more oil if necessary. When they have softened and coloured lightly, pour in the prunes and cider. The cider will bubble up, so take care. Leave to simmer until reduced by about half. Add the cream and simmer to thicken slightly, then check the seasoning. Return the pork to the pan with the thyme and heat through. Don't allow the pork to cook any longer, as it will toughen.

pork chops with chicory and lemon

This is ideal for a large fatty chop from a rare breed pig such as Tamworth or Gloucester Old Spot. The lemon juice is the key ingredient for a great sauce when combined with the meat juices, while the chicory adds a lovely bitter flavour. Chicory is a much underused vegetable; also known as Belgian endive, it has tightly packed crisp white leaves with yellow or pale green edges. You may need to trim off some of the outer leaves if they are a little brown at the edges and take a very thin slice off the base, but make sure the chicory stays in one piece.

SERVES 2

2 x 225 g/8 oz pork chops
1 tbsp sunflower oil
25 g/1 oz butter
2 heads of chicory,
  trimmed and sliced in half
  lengthways
50 ml/2 fl oz dry white wine
juice of 1 small lemon
salt and pepper

Dry the chops with absorbent kitchen paper. Remove the skin and then make deep slashes – say three or four – through the fat almost to the meat (this helps to cook the fat quicker). Use a large heavy-based shallow pan with a lid that will hold the chops and chicory in one layer. Add the sunflower oil and heat until hot enough to brown the meat. You can test by just touching a corner of the meat into the pan – if it sizzles, then it's hot enough. Place the chops carefully in the pan, then brown on both sides; this will take a few minutes and the meat will spit. If it gets too hot, lower the temperature a little. Remove the meat from the pan and add the butter, then brown the chicory all over. Reduce the temperature.

Return the pork to the pan, pour in the wine, season with salt and pepper and cover, then simmer gently for 10 minutes, or until you can slide a knife into the chicory easily. Transfer the pork and chicory to a serving dish and keep warm. Pour in the lemon juice and swirl around to combine, then pour over the pork and chicory and serve.

casserole of pork with fresh herbs and ale

I have done lots of outdoor cookery demonstrations and always love using local produce. The idea came about when I was demonstrating in a tent in front of Blair Castle in Perthshire. It was a really windy day and pouring with rain and the tent was packed, but I suspect most people weren't in there to watch me. I was having to shout to be heard above the wind and rain and, just as I was finishing, there was a huge gust and a large amount of water (which had been collecting near an upright pole holding up the tent) was forced through a gap in the roof and poured into the tent. Luckily no one got wet, but it was a dramatic moment. While I was recovering, the man from the Heather Ale stand gave me a glass of this great drink: 'You look as if you might need this,' he said. It's an ale flavoured not with hops but with heather. I loved the floral overtones and felt it would go well with pork. This is the result.

SERVES 4

800 g/1 lb 2oz diced lean
  pork
3 tbsp plain flour seasoned
  with salt and pepper
2 tbsp olive oil
2–3 medium onions,
  peeled and chopped
1 garlic clove, peeled
  and crushed
1 x 500 ml/18 fl oz bottle
  Heather Ale or other
  fragrant ale
2 tbsp chopped fresh
  herbs, such as coriander,
  parsley, chervil, tarragon

Preheat the oven to 180°C/350°F/gas 4.

Dry the pork with absorbent kitchen paper, then toss it in the seasoned flour and shake off any excess flour. Heat a large frying pan and add the olive oil. Brown the meat in batches, to keep the heat in the pan, adding more oil if necessary. It is important to keep the temperature high to prevent the pork from exuding its moisture.

Once all the meat has been browned, put it into a casserole dish. Reduce the heat, add the onions and garlic to the frying pan, allow to soften and brown lightly, then add to the meat. Pour a little water into the pan, scrape up the bits left by the browning pork and pour over the pork. Pour the ale into the casserole to just cover the meat, then bring to the boil. Cover with a lid and cook in the oven for about 1½ hours. About 5 minutes before the end of cooking time, add the chopped herbs. If the liquid is too thin, lift out the pork with a slotted spoon and allow the liquid to bubble, uncovered, on the hob for a few minutes until it thickens slightly. Serve with mashed potatoes.

pork with plums

One September, I had lots of plums on my trees at home and was thinking of ways to use them seasonally. The Heather Ale referred to on the previous page comes into its own again here. But, of course, if you have a local fragrant ale to hand, then use that.

SERVES 4

2 x 250 g/9 oz pork fillets
1 tbsp honey
1 garlic clove, peeled and
  crushed
175 ml/6 fl oz Heather Ale
  or other fragrant ale
1 sprig of rosemary
8–12 plums, ripe but firm
2–3 tbsp butter
1 tsp caster sugar, to taste
2 tsp olive oil

Cut the pork into strips. Combine the honey, garlic, ale and rosemary in a bowl, add the pork and leave to marinate for up to 30 minutes.

Prepare the plums by removing the stones – this is best done by slicing them in half from top to bottom.

Heat a large heavy-based frying pan and add 1 tbsp of the butter and the caster sugar. When the butter has melted, add the plums and cook until lightly caramelised, then set aside. You may have to do this in two batches, adding a little more butter and sugar each time.

Dry the pork pieces on absorbent kitchen paper, retaining the marinade. Heat a wide pan, add the olive oil and 1 tsp of butter and quickly brown the pork pieces all over – do not overcook at this stage, or the pork will become tough. Remove from the pan.

Strain the marinade and add to the pan, then boil to reduce to about 2 tbsp. Return the pork to the pan, add the plums, gently combine and heat through until the pork is cooked. Serve with some steamed rice to mop up the sauce.

pork with creamed leeks

This idea came to me when I was running Portsonachan Hotel on Loch Awe in the west of Scotland. I actually tried it first with a whole loin and roasted it with most of the fat trimmed away, but I love the old Scots word 'collop' and decided to use collops – slices cut from a pork tenderloin – for this recipe. The sweetness of the pork is nicely counterbalanced by the strong leek flavour enriched with the cream. It is a real winter dish; serve with mashed potatoes or perhaps a flat pasta.

SERVES 2

75 g/3 oz butter
2 leeks, trimmed and diced
100 ml/3½ fl oz double cream
1 pork fillet weighing about 250 g/9 oz, cut into 4 pieces
1 tsp groundnut oil or vegetable oil
a dash of dry white wine
150 ml/5 fl oz pork stock (see page 259)
salt and pepper

Prepare the leeks first. Melt 2 tsp of the butter in a saucepan, add the leeks and stir until they wilt. Add the cream and season with salt and pepper, then cook on a medium heat until the mixture thickens. Put on one side.

Dry the pieces of pork on absorbent kitchen paper. Heat a heavy-based pan and pour in the oil and 1 tsp of the butter. When the pan is hot, quickly sear the pork on all sides to colour them all over, then reduce the heat and continue to cook gently for about 5 minutes, until just cooked – do not overcook, or the pork will be tough. Remove the pork and keep warm.

Deglaze the pan with white wine, then add the stock, bring to a rapid boil and reduce to about 2 tbsp of liquid. Take off the heat and swirl in the remaining butter until melted; do not put back on the heat.

Serve the creamed leeks in the middle of a large plate with the collops of pork resting against them and a swirl of sauce over the whole.

loin of pork with lemon and mushroom sauce

This is a real Sunday lunch-type dish – the pork will sit quite happily for a while, as will the sauce, and there is no last-minute rush of things to do. The sauce is slightly old-fashioned in its use of flour as a base, but it is very homely and marries well with the pork. You can use button mushrooms or a mix of any you may pick wild, such as field mushrooms.

SERVES 6–8

2 kg/4½ lb piece of pork loin off the bone, without skin
300 g/11 oz button or field mushrooms, sliced
100 g/3½ oz butter
50 g/2 oz plain flour
500 ml/18 fl oz milk, seasoned with salt and pepper
2 tbsp chopped fresh chives or parsley or both, plus extra to serve
finely grated zest of 2 lemons and the juice of 1 lemon
salt and pepper

Preheat the oven to 200°C/400°F/gas 6.

Season the pork with salt and pepper, rubbing it into the fat, then place in a roasting tin and roast for 45 minutes. Reduce the oven temperature to 190°C/375°F/gas 5 and cook for another 30–55 minutes. Check that the pork is cooked by piercing the centre with a fine skewer: the juices should be pale and golden, not pink.

Remove the roasting tin from the oven. Transfer the pork to a carving board, cover with foil and leave to rest while you make the sauce.

Spoon 2 tbsp of the fat from the roasting tin into a saucepan and cook the mushrooms for a few minutes. Remove and keep on one side. Add the butter to the pan and, when melted, stir in the flour for a few minutes to cook, then slowly add the milk to create a smooth but thickish sauce (don't add all the milk if it seems to be getting thin). Stir in the herbs, lemon juice and zest and the mushrooms and check for seasoning.

Just before serving, pour any pork juices sitting in the roasting tin into the pan, as long as they are not too fatty. Slice the pork, spoon the sauce on to partially coat the slices and sprinkle on more chopped chives and/or parsley. Serve with root vegetables and mashed potatoes.

baked chops in foil with apple and honey

Long, slow cooking has come back into fashion as cheaper cuts are being re-assessed. Another technique for keeping food moist and tender is to wrap it in foil or greaseproof paper before baking or steaming. I can remember some classic French chef cooking salmon 'en papillote' and the pleasure of opening your own little parcel at the table and the glorious aroma wafting up of fresh salmon, herbs and wine.

Well, this idea uses foil as the cooking bag. The recipe is straightforward, but you can adapt it for the barbecue or use cheaper cuts and cook overnight in a slow oven. I can never decide if I prefer a dessert apple or a cooker – it's up to you!

SERVES 4

a little olive oil to grease
4 pork chops
1 large apple
4 tsp honey
4 sprigs of marjoram
dry cider (optional)
salt and pepper

Preheat the oven to 180°C/350°F/gas 4.

Take four sheets of foil, each one large enough to fold over and enclose a chop and some apple. Lightly oil the centre of each piece of foil. Dry the pork chops, then brown in a hot pan with a little olive oil for 2 minutes on each side. Place one chop in the middle of each sheet and season lightly with salt and pepper.

Cut the apple into quarters and remove the core, then slice each quarter into five and place on the pork chops. Add 1 tsp of honey to the apples on each chop, then add a sprig of marjoram – a splash of cider at this point adds its own character. Fold the foil over to enclose the contents, place on a baking tray and cook in the oven for about 1 hour. The slower the oven, the longer the cooking, but the more melty the pork!

escalopes of pork with avocado and sage

I based this idea on the Italian *Saltimbocca alla Romana*, in which veal escalopes are topped with Parma ham and sage. The pungent flavour of sage and the creamy texture of avocado blend well with pork. You can use most cuts for this as long as they are relatively fat free and beaten until fairly thin. The avocados must be ripe.

SERVES 4

2 x 250 g/9 oz pork fillets
1 ripe avocado
50 g/2 oz butter
2 tsp roughly chopped
  fresh sage
juice of ½ lemon
salt and pepper

Cut each pork fillet into two pieces across the grain and flatten them between two sheets of clingfilm with the flat of a large knife or a rolling pin. Cut the avocado in half and remove the stone and peel, then carefully slice thinly lengthways.

Melt half the butter in a frying pan over a medium heat. Pat the pork escalopes dry and season with salt and pepper, then add to the pan and cook quickly to colour the pork on both sides – about 3–5 minutes; do not overcook, or the pork will become tough.

Transfer the pork escalopes to four heated plates and place the sliced avocado equally over them. Return the pan to the heat and add the remaining butter and the sage. Stir to collect the juices from the pan and, as the butter darkens slightly, add the lemon juice, then spoon over the pork and serve.

spare ribs

The ribs most associated with barbecuing are from the lower rib cage. A whole rack of ribs usually weighs about 1.3 kg/2¾ lb with 13 ribs. There is very little meat, but what there is, is very succulent. I usually divide them into 3- or 4-rib pieces, each serving one person: this keeps the meat succulent and avoids the problem of individual ribs getting lost on the barbecue.

The idea is to cook them in the oven for 20 minutes or so, then grill them on a low barbecue, and, finally, coat them in sauce and cook a little longer. They can also be cooked entirely in the oven – which is useful in the winter!

Here is the basic method, followed by a few recipe ideas.

SERVES 4

1.6–1.8 kg/3½–4 lb ribs
sauce of your choice
  (see overleaf)

Preheat the oven to 180°C/350°F/gas 4.

Place the ribs on a baking sheet and cook in the oven for 20 minutes, then place on a low barbecue and cook for 30 minutes. Alternatively, continue cooking in the oven for a further 30 minutes. Coat in your prepared sauce and cook for another 15 minutes.

sauces

red pepper

1 tbsp vegetable oil
2 red peppers, deseeded and cut into pieces
6 garlic cloves, peeled and pulped
1 tbsp soy sauce
1 tbsp chopped sundried tomatoes
2 tbsp chopped fresh coriander
black pepper

Heat the vegetable oil in a pan and fry the peppers until they soften. Reduce the heat, add the garlic and cook for a couple of minutes, making sure it doesn't burn.

Add the soy sauce and tomatoes and purée in a food processor. Coat the ribs prior to the final barbecuing or roasting. Sprinkle with the coriander and black pepper to serve.

sweet and sour

1 tbsp olive oil
6 tbsp red wine vinegar
2 tbsp tomato purée
4 tbsp runny honey
1 tbsp wholegrain mustard
2 tbsp soy sauce
2 garlic cloves, peeled and pulped

Mix all the ingredients together and coat the ribs prior to the final barbecuing or roasting.

American

3 tbsp vegetable oil
1 onion, peeled and chopped
1–2 sticks of celery, chopped
3 garlic cloves, peeled and pulped
175 ml/6 fl oz wine vinegar
2 tbsp tomato purée
125 ml/4 fl oz water
1 tbsp black treacle
40 g/1^1/$_2$ oz brown sugar
2 tbsp Worcestershire sauce
2 tsp hot paprika
1 tsp mustard
^{1}/$_2$ tsp black pepper
^{1}/$_2$ tsp cayenne pepper
salt

Heat the vegetable oil in a large pan, then add the onion, celery and garlic and stew until soft.

Add all the remaining ingredients and simmer until quite thick. Blend in a food processor to produce a smooth sauce. Coat the ribs prior to the final barbecuing or roasting.

what is bacon?

Bacon comes from the belly, back and loin of the pig and is cured by salting and/or smoking. The word 'bacon' means 'meat from the back of an animal' and is believed to come from prehistoric German '*bak*', which was also the source of the English word 'back'. For many hundreds of years, a salt-cured and smoked piece of the pig sustained poor families throughout the winter and was frequently the only meat available. The salted or smoked meat was often added to soups and stews.

The type of pig kept and its diet depended on whether it was intended for fresh pork or bacon. Pigs for bacon were typically heavier. Some breeds, such as Tamworth, were specially bred for bacon; nowadays the same breed of pig is often used for both fresh and cured meat, but bacon pigs are killed at a heavier weight than those for fresh pork, usually at around 100 kg (220 lb). The slaughtered pig would be hung for a day, then cured to preserve it through the winter. The cure could be plain, sweet (with honey) or spiced. The sides of bacon, shimmering with salt, were hung from the rafters to mature and later could be hung in the chimney and smoked. Unsmoked bacon is also known as 'green' bacon.

Bacon comes in a wide variety of cuts and flavours (according to the cure). Cuts include streaky, back and middle, as well as bacon chops and joints. Streaky bacon comes from the belly of the pig and is quite fatty; back bacon has less fat, while middle bacon is streaked with fat, but is leaner than streaky. Gammon is the word used for the raw, cured hind leg of a pig removed from a side of bacon (a 'side' of bacon means half the carcass, divided lengthwise). The word 'gammon' comes from the Old French *gambon* (from *gambe*, 'leg').

CURING

Bacon can be wet- or dry-cured. Wet-cured bacon is immersed in a brine tub with salts, spices, sugar and other seasonings. Other liquid may also be added: apple juice, beer or cider, for example. Sweet-cured bacon has honey, maple syrup, black treacle or sugar added. Dry-cured bacon is rubbed with a mixture of salts and spices and then hung to dry and mature for a period of time, which varies according to the producer.

A combination of different types of salt was frequently used, such as a mixture of coarse sea salt, rock salt and bay salt (originally from the Bay of Biscay, although later this term meant sea salt). Fine salt would seal the meat too quickly before it penetrated into the flesh, but coarse salt dissolves more slowly and permeates the meat. Large flaked Maldon salt from Essex was regarded as particularly good for curing. Saltpetre has been used in curing since the Middle Ages to kill bacteria; it also gives the meat a pink colour. Since the mid-nineteenth century, sodium nitrate has been used for the same purpose; it is needed in smaller amounts than potassium nitrate. Salprunella, a reduced form of saltpetre, is also sometimes used sparingly.

The cure is important to the flavour of the finished product, and the types of cure vary according to region and are distinctively different. Today many producers have their own secret curing recipes, which often include herbs, spices and sugar. Today's cures are milder than those of the past.

After the curing process, bacon may also be cold-smoked – food has been preserved by smoking since antiquity. After first being salted, meat and fish were hung in huts and caves, where smoke from the cooking fires pervaded the flesh. The smoke penetrates the food to impart the characteristic smoky flavour, while tarry substances in wood smoke kill bacteria and form an airtight seal on the surface of the food. Smoking gives bacon rind a dark golden hue. Nowadays cold-smoking, in a kiln or smokehouse, is done at a temperature below 30°C/86°F to avoid cooking the food, but to allow the food to change in colour, flavour and texture. The choice of wood for smoking is a major factor in the taste of the finished product – oak, beech, hickory and maple are the most popular.

These days, many large-scale commercially smoked foods are produced in factories, with less smoking time than the traditional product (to reduce weight loss) and the use of dyes to simulate the appearance of a product smoked for a longer period. Other foods described as 'smoke flavour' have a chemical added to give a smoky taste, instead of being smoked over wood.

Large-scale, commercial bacon production is thought to have started in the eighteenth century: in 1770, John Harris of Calne in Wiltshire had the idea that slaughtering and curing pigs on the spot would be more practical than the previous practice of driving pigs to London's curing houses on foot – often a long and exhausting journey, which spoiled their meat. The Wiltshire cure was subsequently developed by the Harris family in the 1840s and was groundbreaking at the time, as the meat was cured in rooms chilled by ice. The Harris family discovered that much less salt was needed to cure their bacon and hams in these cool conditions, and so a milder cure was born. Sides of pork are immersed in brine for 3–4 days, then put into a cool cellar for two weeks to mature and then smoked over oak, pine or beech wood for 2–3 days.

Another popular cure is sweet black bacon, or Suffolk sweet-cured bacon, which is dry-cured with salt and molasses sugar for six weeks, then smoked over oak; the salty deep-pink bacon has a distinctively sweet flavour, with a hint of rich, dark treacly molasses.

Ayrshire bacon is made in southwest Scotland, traditionally from Large White pigs, and is a very lightly salted mild cure that originated in 1857 and is still very popular throughout Scotland. Pig farming was predominant in the county, and the preference there has always been for cured rather than fresh pork. After curing, the rind is removed and the meat is tightly rolled and tied with string – which ensures that the fat and lean meat are evenly distributed – before it is cut into rashers. It may be smoked or unsmoked.

Modern, intensively reared bacon pigs are fed on a low-fat diet and have almost no exercise. Their meat is usually 'cured' by being injected with brine and phosphates to plump it up and increase its weight, but as a consequence, this type of bacon releases a white liquid during cooking and shrinks alarmingly in the pan. It is definitely worth paying more and buying traditionally cured bacon from free-range pigs, smoked in the time-honoured way to ensure the best flavour and texture.

Two other British regional cured pork products are worth mentioning:

✱ The Bath Chap is a boned, cured and cooked pig's cheek. This is an old English delicacy, although why it was particularly associated with the city of Bath is unclear. The word 'chap' is a variant on 'chop', a term from the sixteenth century that denoted the jaws and cheek of an animal. In the traditional preparation, the cooked Bath Chaps are pressed in a mould to give them their characteristic cone shape, then removed when cold and dusted with breadcrumbs. They were very popular in the nineteenth century, when they were commonly called simply 'chaps'. Bath Chaps must be made from a long-jawed pig, such as the dappled Gloucester Old Spot, which used to be fed on windfall apples from the region's many apple orchards, said to give the meat a unique flavour. (Pigs adore apples.) Bath Chaps fell out of favour and seemed to almost disappear for a time, but the speciality has been revived in the Bath region and appears on restaurant menus, served hot or cold. (See page 234.)

✳ Cured chine is made from a section of the pig between the shoulder blades, cut through the backbone. This was traditional in East Anglia and Lincolnshire and was often served at celebrations such as weddings, christenings and at harvest time. The cured meat was slashed deeply from the fat to the bone and the stuffing, made from green herbs, particularly parsely, packed into the slashes before it was baked or boiled. It made an attractive centrepiece because, when it was sliced, the pink meat contrasted with the white fat and bright green herbs. Cured chine was usually served cold with vinegar. It is available today only as a speciality in Lincolnshire.

AN ANCIENT CUSTOM

Bacon is the subject of an ancient English custom. Every four years in Great Dunmow, Essex, the Dunmow Flitch Trials award a flitch of bacon (half a pig, cut lengthwise) to married couples from anywhere in the world, if they can satisfy the judge and jury of six maidens and six bachelors that in 'twelvemonth and a day' they have 'not wisht themselves unmarried again'. It is believed that the custom originated in 1104 at the Augustinian Priory of Little Dunmow. The Lord of the Manor, Reginald Fitzwalter, and his wife dressed themselves as humble folk and begged the blessing of the Prior a year and a day after their marriage. The Prior, pleased by such devotion, presented them with a flitch of bacon. Fitzwalter then revealed his true identity and gave his land to the Priory on the condition that a flitch be awarded to any married couple who could claim they were similarly devoted. The Dunmow Flitch Trials subsequently became famous throughout England.

The earliest record of a successful claimant to the Dunmow Flitch was in 1445, when Richard Wright travelled from Norwich and won the bacon. The win is recorded in documents from the Priory of Little Dunmow, held by the British Museum.

After the Reformation, the awarding of the Flitch was taken over by the Lord of the Manor, but over the years the custom lapsed. Victorian novelist Harrison Ainsworth is credited with reviving the Trials as an entirely civic event. In 1855, following the publication of his popular novel *The Custom of Dunmow*, in which Ainsworth recounts the attempts by Little Dunmow's publican to win the flitch by marrying a succession of wives in an attempt to find the perfect one, the Trials were once again staged in Great Dunmow. They have been held regularly ever since and, from the end of the Second World War, every four years, in a leap year. Successful couples are carried shoulder-high by bearers in the ancient flitch chair to the Market Place, where they take the oath (similar to pre-Reformation marriage vows) kneeling on pointed stones. Unsuccessful couples have to walk behind the empty chair to the Market Place, but are consoled with a prize of gammon.

The original custom of awarding a flitch to those who can prove marital harmony is not unique to Dunmow. There are references from across Europe to similar customs, now long abandoned. However, the town is unique in continuing to reward marital harmony with a Flitch of Bacon well into the twenty-first century.

AN INTERNATIONAL FAVOURITE

There's an old English saying, 'to bring home the bacon', which means to succeed or win a prize. Centuries ago, a pig was the most sought-after prize at fairs around the country. Bowling for a pig was a skittles competition, where the best score won a piglet. A more energetic game was trying to catch a greased pig. The winner was given a pig to take home.

In Ireland bacon, as well as fresh pork and other products of the pig, has long been an important part of the country's economy and, in the past, the major bacon-curing centres were Waterford, Limerick, Cork and Belfast. Pigs for the Belfast market were killed on the farm and arrived as carcasses, while those sent to the other markets were despatched alive to be killed and cured. Enniscorthy in County Wexford was once famous for its 'barley-fed bacon', usually bought as a joint and boiled. The pigs were fed on a barley-enriched diet and grew faster and had thicker back fat than other pigs. *Bagun bruite* (boiled bacon), a piece cut from the shoulder, collar or flitch and served with cabbage, was once a culinary staple, particularly at harvest time, and remains very popular in Ireland today.

The French word for bacon is *lard*, or *lardons* if diced, and is derived from the Latin *lardum* (bacon fat). A rasher of bacon is called a *tranche de lard*; streaky bacon (from the belly) is known as *lard de poitrine* or, if smoked, as *poitrine fumée*. Very lean bacon (from the loin) is called *bacon*.

Overleaf: Bacon and sausages hanged for drying and smoking at the Open-Air-Museum Ballenberg, Brienz, Switzerland.

Ventrèche (meaning 'belly') from southwest France comes from the part of the pig's belly where the muscles are separated by strips of fat. It can be sliced thinly, seared and used in salads or canapés, or used to wrap lean meat, poultry or shellfish, particularly scallops, to add flavour and moistness. There are two types of *ventrèche*, each cured in a different way. *Ventrèche salée* (salted *ventrèche*), the more common, is salted for 10 days, then washed, seasoned with crushed pepper and dried for up to four weeks. *Ventrèche fumée* (smoked *ventrèche*) is not salted, but is cured by smoking.

Italian *pancetta* comes from the belly of the pig (*pancia*), but has a completely different flavour from British streaky bacon, as it is cured in a different way. *Pancetta* is salt-cured and spiced, often with fennel, pepper and nutmeg, and is an important ingredient of many Italian dishes, such as minestrone soup, Bolognese sauce and spaghetti carbonara (see page 96). (The latter may be a reference to the *carbonari* – charcoal burners, who could make this dish quickly. An alternative theory is that the recipe is fairly new and was inspired by the American GIs and their bacon and egg rations, since it contains both.) *Pancetta curata* is salt-cured or air-dried; *pancetta arrotolata* (rolled *pancetta*) is lean and spiced with peppercorns and cloves, and is served very thinly sliced as part of an antipasto; *rigatino pancetta* from Tuscany is also served very thinly sliced; *pancetta stesa* is the belly left flat – it may be cured with herbs and it is used in cooking as a flavouring ingredient; *pancetta affumicata* is smoked and is used in many northern Italian dishes.

Guanciale (from *guancia*, cheek) is pig's cheek rubbed with salt, ground black pepper or red pepper and then cured for three weeks. It has a more pronounced flavour than *pancetta* and its texture is more delicate. It is a speciality of central Italy and is particularly popular in Umbria and Lazio.

Tocino is the Spanish term for bacon, which is usually unsmoked; if smoked, it is usually called *bacon*. *Tocino Ibérico* is a gourmet bacon, made from pigs fed on acorns and it has a wonderful flavour; it is sliced thinly and normally served warm. Spain also makes a version of *pancetta*, called *tocino de panceta*, pork belly that has been salt-cured, salted and spiced, then dried for about three months. It appears as a side dish, usually fried in olive oil or in its own fat, and in some rural areas is popular served with fried eggs and *chorizo* for breakfast.

In Germany, bacon is known generally as *Speck*; it usually means streaky bacon or just the fat. It is generally assumed that *Speck* is smoked, but there is also *Grüner Speck* – uncured pork belly, which is cooked like other raw meat. *Speck* originated in the Tyrol region on the borders of Italy and Austria and has the distinctive flavour of juniper. It was first recorded in the Middle Ages and *Speck dell'Alto Adige* (*Südtiroler Speck*) now has European PGI status (Protected Geographical Indication), which assures the integrity and reputation of foods with an identified geographical origin. A leg of pork is boned and cured in a mixture of salt, herbs and spices (including juniper berries); it is then cold-smoked over beech wood (the wood determines much of the flavour) before being air-dried to mature for five months. It is often served cut into wafer-thin slices and accompanied by strong flavours such as dark rye bread, pickles and horseradish.

Bauchspeck comes from the pork belly and is the bacon used for cooking. *Bauchspeck* is usually sold in pieces: the '*schwarte*' (rind) is removed first and the pieces are then diced and browned in the pan. *Schinkenspeck*, a cured and smoked cut of pork from the back hip, is sliced thinly and usually served cold. It has larger muscles and less marbling than the inexpensive *Speck* used for cooking.

Schwarzwälder Speck (Black Forest bacon) is cured in a spiced brine, then smoked over pine wood until black on the outside. Locally it is often enjoyed with a thick slice of country bread and a glass of kirsch.

In Hungary a reddish-coloured, paprika-coated, hearty slab bacon is eaten with country bread and raw onion or raw garlic; spicy *Ciganyszalonna* ('gypsy' bacon) is smoked and is usually served in thin slices with rye bread. (In Germany it is known as *Zigeunerspeck*.)

THE RECIPES

steamed pork, bacon and leek pudding

I have to acknowledge the great Simon Hopkinson for this recipe. It comes from his wonderful book *Roast Chicken and Other Stories – Second Helpings*. Simon is an intuitive cook and, like another of my heroes, Nigel Slater, has the ability to conjure up amazing food images as well as get the recipes down on paper. I have found it a good idea to add some chopped herbs, such as summer savory, to the pastry. It's traditional to serve the pudding wrapped in a linen napkin, and spoon it out from the basin.

SERVES 4–6

FOR THE DOUGH
300 g/11 oz self-raising flour
150 g/5 oz shredded suet
chopped fresh herbs (optional)
a little oil to grease
salt and pepper

FOR THE FILLING
2 tbsp plain flour
2 tsp chopped sage
250 g/9 oz pork belly without skin, cut into 2 cm/³/₄ inch chunks
50 g/2 oz lean bacon, chopped quite finely
1 pig's kidney, core removed and chopped quite finely
2 leeks, trimmed, sliced and washed
2 tbsp sherry
100 ml/3¹/₂ fl oz water
salt and pepper

Mix the flour, suet and seasoning with the herbs, if using, in a large bowl and add enough water to achieve a moist dough. Knead for a few minutes to make it supple – it should not be too dry, but it shouldn't be sticky either. Set aside.

For the filling, season the flour with salt, pepper and sage, and toss the chunks of pork through it, then add the bacon, kidney and leeks with the sherry and water. Mix well together.

Grease a 1 litre/1¾ pint pudding basin with the oil. Roll out two-thirds of the dough, enough to line the bowl with a little overhang, and place in the basin. Put in the filling, pushing down evenly but not so hard that it breaks the dough. Roll out the remaining dough to make a lid, then cover the filling. Dampen the edges and squeeze together, trim off the excess and make a small hole in the middle of the lid. Cover with a sheet of greased greaseproof paper with a central pleat, then cover with a sheet of foil and secure with string. Steam for 2–3 hours.

Asturian bean stew

Beans have been the staple of many peoples around the world. I always think of Westerns in which the cowboys would eat their pork and beans around the campfire. In Brazil, rice and beans with a little bit of bacon are eaten almost every day. The Spanish have long incorporated beans into their food and the surrealist film director Luis Buñuel is purported to have said, rather cuttingly, that 'this is a dish discovered by a nation of hungry people'. For me, it represents a truly economical meal.

SERVES 6

500 g/1 lb 2oz unsmoked
  bacon or gammon joint
400 g/14 oz large dried
  white beans (*fabes*)
2 tbsp olive oil
150 g/5 oz smoked streaky
  bacon, cut into lardons
  (see page 87)
1 onion, peeled and
  chopped
1 garlic clove, peeled and
  chopped
1 bay leaf
a few saffron threads
$1/2$ tsp sweet paprika
2 Spanish blood sausages
  (*morcilla*), about
  100 g/$3^1/2$ oz each
2 whole chorizo sausages,
  about 100 g/$3^1/2$ oz each
salt and black pepper

You need to start this the day before. Soak the bacon in cold water overnight, changing the water at least once to remove the salt. Soak the beans in cold water overnight.

The next day, heat the olive oil in a large casserole, then add the streaky bacon and onion and cook until softened. Add the garlic and stir through. Drain the meat and beans and add to the casserole with enough fresh water to cover. Add the bay leaf, saffron, paprika and pepper and bring to the boil, then simmer on a medium heat for 1½ hours, stirring occasionally.

When the beans are almost soft, add all the sausages and simmer for 30 minutes.

Lift the sausages out, cut into chunks and return to the casserole. Check for seasoning, then serve.

spaghetti carbonara

Pasta is too large an area for me to cover in this book and, of course, there are many pasta dishes with pork products in them, so I thought I would offer just one of the most classic.

SERVES 4

2 garlic cloves, peeled
  and halved
4 tbsp olive oil
200 g/7 oz pancetta or
  unsmoked streaky bacon,
  cut into small lardons
2 whole eggs and 2 egg
  yolks
75 g/3 oz freshly grated
  Parmesan
400 g/14 oz spaghetti
salt and pepper

Fill a large pan with water, add salt and bring to the boil.

Put the garlic and olive oil in a small pan and leave to infuse over a low heat for about 10 minutes. Discard the garlic, add the pancetta or bacon and cook gently until it begins to crisp.

Meanwhile, when the water comes to a rolling boil, lower the spaghetti into the pan, pushing it down as it softens. Give it a good stir. Once the water comes back to the boil, the spaghetti will take about 7 minutes to cook. Check after 5 minutes, it should just have a slight bite to it.

Beat the eggs and yolks together in a large serving bowl, then add about half the Parmesan and some salt and pepper.

Drain the cooked spaghetti and tip into the bowl with the eggs, add the hot pancetta and garlic oil and turn the pasta in the egg mixture. The eggs will cook in the heat. Serve in warmed bowls and hand round the remaining Parmesan for guests to sprinkle on.

Ragged Jack kale with smoked bacon and Anster cheese

This is as much to do with my Fife roots and my passion for kale as anything. I have suggested Ragged Jack simply because it's not the normal kind of kale. You can use the more common curly kale or the more glamorous black kale, which is also known as cavalo nero. I have used Anster cheese since it is the only cheese made in Fife, but any well-flavoured Cheddar or Cheshire type will do. This is a very simple, nutritious supper dish.

PER PERSON

100–150 g/3½–5 oz Ragged Jack, common curly or black kale
a knob of butter or a little virgin olive oil
25 g/1 oz smoked bacon, diced
25 g/1 oz Anster cheese or strongly flavoured Cheddar or Cheshire cheese, shaved or diced
pepper

Trim away the coarse stalks from the kale and roughly shred the leaves. Wash thoroughly and drain but leave slightly wet.

In a frying pan, melt the butter or olive oil and when it is hot add the bacon and cook quickly until lightly browned, then add the kale. Season with pepper and mix through to heat the kale. Put a lid on the pan and leave for a few minutes.

Remove the pan from the heat and allow to rest for another few minutes, then remove the lid, return the pan to the heat and stir gently to heat through and allow the moisture to evaporate.

To serve, pile the kale on a warm plate and add the cheese.

leek and smoked bacon risotto

There are so many variations of risotto – most of which can be made with barley instead of rice. Somehow, the combination of smoked bacon and leek works well with rice, but why not try it with barley for a change? If you do, you will need to cook it for a little longer.

SERVES 4

1.5 litres/2½ pints chicken stock
2 tbsp olive oil
200 g/7 oz smoked bacon, cut into small lardons (see page 87)
2 leeks, trimmed, diced and washed
400 g/14 oz arborio rice
125 ml/4 fl oz dry white wine
1 tbsp unsalted butter
50 g/2 oz Parmesan cheese, grated
salt and black pepper

Heat the stock to boiling point and keep just simmering. Heat the oil in a heavy-based pan over a medium heat, add the bacon and cook until lightly browned. Add the leeks and cook gently until softened. Add the rice and stir well to coat with all the ingredients. Pour in the wine and stir until it has been absorbed.

Now begin to add the stock, a ladleful at a time, stirring constantly and making sure that the liquid is all absorbed before adding the next ladleful. The rice should be tender but still firm to bite – add water if you run out of stock before this moment is reached. This should all take about 20 minutes.

Take off the heat and season to taste, then stir in the butter and cheese and serve.

SALADS

The crisp freshness of a salad is a natural accompaniment to all parts of the pig. A classic, simple green salad with a terrine is a good place to start, and as there are so many leaves to choose from it's often easier to buy a ready mixed bag. My local organic farmshop, Pillars of Hercules in Falkland, sells a seasonal mixture with a variety of leaves and herbs, which changes all the time and in the main is what I base my salads on. But every so often you will want a leaf-specific salad, such as cos/romaine for a Caesar salad, or lamb's lettuce with a confit of duck. The dressing is as important as the leaves and my rule of thumb is for three parts oil to one part vinegar, but of course this, as with the leaves, is open to variation.

A more recent development has been the emergence of salads as a satellite to the main course or even as a main course on their own. A salad does not necessarily have to have lettuce in it, just lovely fresh or lightly blanched vegetables with a dressing to cut through the rich extras.

PREPARING SALADS

I once stayed in a French home where my hostess used to carefully wash her salad leaves and dry them gently by dabbing with a towel. She never shook the leaves in a colander or spun them in a salad drier, but treated them with such tenderness, it was as if each leaf was a loved one and, in a sense, it was. She felt that she became everything she ate and so, to respect herself and those she fed, all the food needed to be treated this way. As you can imagine, meal preparation took a long time! You may say life is too short to pat dry a lettuce leaf, and I agree, but spare a thought for Madame as you spin your leaves dry. Anyway, it is important to wash your leaves and dry them well, so that they don't dilute the dressing. Generally, the leaves should be torn into bite-size pieces.

frisée and bacon

This is unashamedly borrowed from one of my favourite writers, Nigel Slater, who describes it as, 'Probably the best salad in the world. Probably.'

SERVES 4

2 thick slices of good bread
200 g/7 oz bacon
  (whatever rashers you
  have), cut into lardons
4 large handfuls of frisée
  (curly endive)

**FOR THE VINAIGRETTE
  DRESSING**
2 tbsp Dijon mustard
2 tbsp red wine vinegar
100 ml/3^1/$_2$ fl oz groundnut
  oil or light olive oil
salt and pepper

Cut the bread into squares slightly larger than the length of the lardons.

For the vinaigrette dressing, whisk the mustard, vinegar and most of the oil with salt and pepper to form a dressing.

In a frying pan, cook the bacon bits in a little oil, over a high heat. As they start to colour, add the cubes of bread and cook until crisp.

Use only the crispiest, curliest, brown-edge free bits of frisée and toss in a bowl with the dressing. Add the bacon and croutons (for that is what they are now called) and toss through. Serve warm.

salad of bitter greens with poached eggs and prosciutto

Eggs and prosciutto make a fine counterpoint to the strongly flavoured leaves. I tend not to eat salads in the winter because I never know how the leaves are produced at that time of year, but this is the exception to my rule. Batavia, also known as escarole, is a type of chicory; it's slightly less bitter than its relations, frisée (curly endive) and radicchio. Frisée could be used here, as could green cabbage, and red cabbage could replace the radicchio.

SERVES 4

4 free-range eggs
1 tbsp wine vinegar
400 g/14 oz batavia
   (escarole), shredded
50 g/2 oz radicchio, finely
   shredded
115 g/4 oz prosciutto,
   thinly sliced

FOR THE SHALLOT
   VINAIGRETTE
2 shallots, peeled and finely
   chopped
1 tbsp balsamic vinegar
1 garlic clove, peeled and
   finely chopped
1 tsp Dijon mustard
50 ml/2 fl oz extra virgin
   olive oil
salt and pepper

For the shallot vinaigrette, whisk the shallots with the vinegar, garlic and mustard, then whisk in the olive oil in a steady stream to form an emulsified dressing. Check for seasoning.

Poach the eggs: bring a wide, shallow, pan of water to the boil and add the vinegar. Reduce the heat to a gentle simmer. Carefully break your eggs, one at a time, into a cup (or use four cups). Using a spoon, stir the water to create a sort of whirlpool in the pan, then drop each egg into the middle of the whirlpool. This, combined with the vinegar, will keep the whites around the yolk. Poach for about 3 minutes, then remove with a slotted spoon and drain on absorbent kitchen paper.

Dress the leaves and place in four bowls. Place a warm poached egg in each one and drape slices of prosciutto over the top. Serve warm.

other variations

salad with potato and mustard dressing

12 small waxy potatoes, such as Belle de fontaney,
  maris peers or pink fir apple
1 egg yolk
1 tsp Dijon mustard
1 tsp wholegrain mustard
100 ml/3^1/$_2$ fl oz wine vinegar
300 ml/^{1}/$_2$ pint rapeseed oil
a handful of small salad leaves,
  such as red chard, tatsoi or mizuna
salt and black pepper

Cook the potatoes and keep warm. In a bowl,
whisk the egg yolk with the mustards, then
gradually add the vinegar to combine. Slowly
dribble the rapeseed oil in, whisking all the time.
Season with salt and pepper.

Cut the warm potatoes up and mix with the
leaves and dressing.

salsa verde

2 shallots peeled and finely chopped
1 tbsp capers, chopped
1 tbsp herbs such as parsley, tarragon chervil
  and chives, chopped
^{1}/$_3$ cucumber deseeded and chopped
clove of garlic, chopped
up to 2 tsbp olive oil or rape seed oil
salt and pepper

Combine all ingredients using enough of the oil
to hold it together. Season to taste.

prosciutto with fruits

Prosciutto has a flavour all of its own, but
wrapped around quarters of a juicy, ripe pear
(from which you have cut out the core) it serves
as a perfect first course. Or, try delicate ripe
orange-fleshed melon (not honeydew) with thin
slices of prosciutto draped over. Prosciutto
works very well with the delicate flavour of figs.
Need I say more?

Dean & Deluca croque signor

This is my take on a great idea for a slightly different croque monsieur. The famous New York deli Dean & Deluca have managed to cast their culinary spell far with their wonderful cookbook, which is one of the most used on my shelves. Its no-nonsense approach to food and incredible knowledge have given me hours of reading pleasure. One day I will make it into their place and buy one of these.

MAKES 2 CROQUES

4 x 7.5 cm/3 inch squares
  of focaccia, cut 2.5 cm/
  1 inch thick
225 g/8 oz mozzarella,
  cut into thin slices
115 g/4 oz prosciutto,
  cut very thin
1 sprig of fresh oregano
  or marjoram
olive oil

Take two squares of focaccia and place half the mozzarella over them. Top with the prosciutto, then the oregano or marjoram and then with the rest of the mozzarella. Cover with the remaining two focaccia slices.

Heat a large frying pan and add a little olive oil, then brown the sandwiches on both sides – the cheese should be melted and the prosciutto lightly warmed. Serve while still hot.

BLT

MAKES 4 SANDWICHES

1 romaine lettuce
3–4 ripe tomatoes
12 rashers of middle
  cut bacon
8 slices of medium-cut
  good-quality white bread
home-made or good-quality
  mayonnaise
black pepper

The quintessential American sandwich, which seems easy but can be fantastic if a few simple procedures are followed and proper heed is given to ingredients. It's not just any old bread or lettuce, it has to be made with the right kind and then you can't go wrong.

Preheat the grill. Break up and wash the lettuce, then drain, dry and set aside.

Slice the tomatoes thinly – you need three slices per sandwich.

Grill the bacon until crispy – this is where a good middle or half streaky and half back is perfect. Set aside. Toast the bread until light brown.

To assemble, place four slices of toast on the board and spread with the mayonnaise. Place the shredded romaine on in a light layer, then the tomato and season with black pepper, then place the bacon, trying to keep any bits from sticking out. Place the last four pieces of toast on top and press down firmly. Trim the edges of any excess bits of bacon or lettuce, but not the crust, then slice the sandwiches in two diagonally, opening each one up to show the layers. Serve on a plate. The cook gets to eat the trimmed bits! Eat and repeat.

MAKES 4 SANDWICHES

12 cherry tomatoes
Olive oil
Sea salt
8 slices of bread, of choice
8 rashers of bacon
80 g/3 oz feta cheese,
  cut into small cubes
  or thin slices

BACON, MUSHROOM & MOSTARDA

I have tried this with both toasted and un-toasted bread – both work well. Mostarda is a wonderful condiment originally from Italy made with dried fruit and a little mustard. It goes well with cheese and cold meats but is delicious in this combination.

MAKES 4 SANDWICHES

4 flat mushrooms
8 rashers of bacon
Mostarda
Olive oil
8 slices of bread, of choice

Trim the stalks from the mushrooms and wipe clean with kitchen paper, place on a grill tray, stalk up, season with some salt and black pepper and a little olive oil. Cook under a high grill for 5 minutes or in a hot oven. Grill the bacon to your liking.

Place 4 slices of bread on a board and spread a teaspoon of Mostarda on each one. Place the mushroom in the middle then cut the bacon in half and place on the top. Cover with another 4 slices of bread and press down, slice diagonally, serve

BACON, ROAST CHERRY TOMATO & FETA

I think this works best with toast as the tomatoes are then squashed in a lovely sauce. You could replace the feta with any soft cheese – it's a good way to use up leftover bits of cheese, but do make sure that if they are quite strong tasting they don't end up as large pieces or the flavour can spoil the balance!

Place the tomatoes on a grill tray and sprinkle with salt and oil. Cook for 10 minutes under the grill (but not too near the heat, tomatoes need a slow cook to really soften).

Next, place 4 slices of toast on a board and spread the tomatoes over them, the tomatoes will break down when pressed. Cut the bacon in half through the middle and place the 4 pieces on each slice, then add the cheese. Season with black pepper and place the top slice of toast on top. Press down firmly and cut in two diagonally. Fresh herbs such as flat parsley oregano or marjoram are always delicious with tomatoes, if using sprinkle on just for the last few minutes of cooking so they don't burn.

what is ham?

Ham is the hind leg of a pig, cured by salting and drying and, sometimes, by smoking. This often lengthy preservation process ensures that the ham can be stored without the need for refrigeration. The practice dates back to the ancient world when meat had to be preserved for a long period and salting was the only way to keep the flesh of animals for any length of time without spoiling. By the Middle Ages, variations on the process had spread throughout Europe, giving rise to countless varieties of ham.

Every ham has its own unique texture and flavour; some regional styles have become world famous. Some hams, such as Parma ham from Italy and *jamón Ibérico* from Spain, are intended to be eaten raw and are served in very thin slices; some, such as England's York ham, will be cooked before sale. Other raw hams are sold ready to be cooked at home and these can be boiled or baked. An old English method of cooking ham was to first enclose it in a flour and water crust, to protect it from the fierce heat of the oven. Another old country cooking method was to simmer the ham in a large pan with a bunch of sweet hay. This reduced the saltiness and imparted a delicate, slightly sweet flavour to the meat.

Unfortunately, some modern commercially produced hams are recognisable by their bright pink colour, wet flabby texture and salty taste, with little discernible flavour. The meat is first injected with water (pork can absorb 75 per cent of its weight in moisture). It is then put into a mechanical tumbler (a drum that rotates slowly) with water or crushed ice and 'tumbled', left to rest, then tumbled again. The process adds weight to the meat, which must be sold as 'water added', as the water makes up part of the weight. Most countries regulate how much water may be added. The meat is then reconstituted and moulded into shape, then cooked and sliced.

Traditionally cured hams, although more expensive, are far superior and have a pleasant texture and rich, intense flavour that is well worth the extra cost.

THE DIFFERENT VARIETIES OF HAM

All hams are salted, either by dry-salting or in brine or a combination of both, and a small quantity of saltpetre (potassium nitrate or sodium nitrate) is added to prevent bacterial infection and give the meat a good pink colour. The meat is left for anything from a few days to several months, then removed from the salt and hung to dry; it may also be smoked over aromatic wood such as pine, oak or hickory.

Hams have been made in Europe for centuries. The type of ham and the differences in flavour and texture are due to the breed of pig and the curing and storage methods used. Some hams are also smoked.

Great Britain

Britain has several internationally renowned hams, prized for their flavour and succulence. They were created in the days when every region developed its own particular methods of salting, curing and smoking. Cures were often carefully guarded, their precise ingredients and quantities of herbs and spices kept secret. Before sugar was affordable and widely available, honey was a popular ingredient of some cures since it had the ability to permeate the meat quickly. Other ingredients might include beer, cider, mustard, treacle and vinegar, as well as aromatic spices and herbs. Different woods were used to smoke hams, imparting their distinctive flavour to the meat.

In Britain, hams are often boiled or baked and, after the skin had been stripped off, the fat is coated with breadcrumbs or glazed. It is traditional in England to decorate the fat of a whole cooked ham or ham joint with whole cloves and then glaze it with a mixture of brown sugar, honey, treacle or mustard. In the past, the skin of cooked hams was also 'vandyked' or scalloped – carved with elaborate and decorative shapes before glazing.

Bradenham ham is an unsmoked, uncooked ham that dates back to 1781 and was originally produced by the Bradenham Ham Company

of Wiltshire and is believed to have been named after the last Lord Bradenham of Buckinghamshire. Traditionally, it is dry-cured in salt, saltpetre and brown sugar, then marinated in molasses and spices, including coriander and juniper berries, which give the ham its characteristic flavour, before being hung to mature for up to six months. Inside the glossy black exterior, the meat is sweet, tender and mild. The curing method was exclusive to the Bradenham Ham Company, which was awarded a prestigious Royal Warrant in 1888. The Wiltshire Bacon Company took over the company in 1897 and then, when that company closed, the Harris Bacon Company took over ham production, which was moved to Yorkshire. Some other hams use the same cure, the only difference being that they are not matured for as long. Shropshire black ham, for instance, is aged for three months.

Suffolk hams were developed from the Long Black pigs in the county and were steeped in a wet pickle with Suffolk ale and treacle, then smoked over oak sawdust before hanging. Nowadays the hams may be cured in either beer or cider; the latter has a milder flavour. The hams are first cured with salt, then put into a mixture of salt, brown sugar, treacle and beer or cider for 3–4 weeks and then smoked over oak chippings and hung to mature for several weeks. The rich mahogany-coloured hams have a deep, intense flavour. Emmett's of Peasenhall has been making Suffolk sweet-cured ham for more than 150 years to a recipe that goes back to the early nineteenth century. First it is steeped in Suffolk stout, treacle and raw cane sugar for six weeks (being turned every day), then hot-smoked over oak sawdust for 2–3 days.

Renowned throughout Europe for hundreds of years, York ham is probably the best known of all the English hams. Traditionally, York ham is made from Large White pigs and is dry-cured in salt and brown sugar for about three months, although the maturation period can last up to two years, depending on the producer. The dry-textured deep-red meat is rich and salty and may be smoked or unsmoked. According to folklore, the hams were originally smoked over the oak wood shavings left over from the construction of York Minster. The English cookery writer Hannah Glasse wrote in 1747, wrote that 'Yorkshire is famous for Hams'. By 1817, they had become known as 'York Hams' and the term had become generic, indicating a particular cure rather than the place where they were made. Today, opinion varies on whether the hams should be smoked or not (unsmoked hams are known as 'green' hams) and current producers describe the process as taking 10 weeks. Nowadays, 'York' hams are also made in countries other than England.

France

The ancient Romans prized the salted, smoked hams from Gaul (modern-day France), which were renowned in antiquity for their splendid flavour and texture. The generic term for ham in France is *jambon*. There is an enormous variety of local hams (*jamon du pays*), some raw, air-cured (*jamon cru*), others cooked, others smoked.

Jambon sec (dry-cured ham) is a designation for hams that meet a minimum weight and which have been dry-cured for a minimum of three months. Hams in this category include those from the Ardennes, Auvergne, Bayonne, Lacaune, Najac and Savoie. *Jambon sec supérieur* refers to hams from pigs raised and processed by traditional methods. One example is *Bigorre* ham, which is made from free-range Gascony black pigs, raised in the Pyrenees mountains in France.

Ardennes, in the Champagne-Ardennes département of northeastern France, is famous for its splendid ham, *Jambon d'Ardennes*, which has long been internationally renowned for its texture and very mild, almost sweet flavour. By the beginning of the nineteenth century, the practice of serving ham to travellers in the region had become so common that narrators complained about it in their writings.

French Ardennes ham, in contrast, is salted by hand and then hung to dry for several months. Originally this ham came from just one breed of pig, which foraged in the woods and lived on acorns, chestnuts and wild roots. Today pigs must be born and raised in the département and fed a diet of at least 75 per cent

Understanding the labels

Protected Designation of Origin (PDO), Protected Geographical Indication (PGI) and Traditional Speciality Guaranteed (TSG) are geographical indications defined in European Union law to protect the names of regional foods. The law (enforced within the EU and being gradually extended internationally with non-EU countries) ensures that only products genuinely originating in that region are allowed. The purpose of the law is to protect the reputation of regional foods and remove the unfair competition and misleading of consumers by non-genuine products that may be of inferior quality or of dissimilar flavour.

These laws protect the names of wines, cheeses, hams, sausages, olives, beers, Balsamic vinegar, regional breads, fruits, and vegetables. Foods such as Melton Mowbray pork pies and Parma ham, for example, can be labelled as such only if they come from their designated region.

This system is similar to Appellation systems throughout the world, such as the Appellation d'origine contrôlée (AOC) used in France, the Denominazione di origine controllata (DOC) in Italy, the Denominação de Origem Controlada (DOC) in Portugal, and the Denominación de Origen (DO) in Spain. The EU PDO/PGI system works alongside the system used in the specified country. For instance, in France, some products have both PDO (AOP in French) and AOC classifications, but usually only the AOC classification will be shown.

cereal. Authentic French Ardennes ham is identified by two trademarks – the region's own emblem and the French hexagon. These guarantee that the ham is made from free-range, local pigs that are fed a natural diet and slaughtered according to strict rules that minimise stress for the animals. The hams are rubbed with salt for several weeks, in order to draw off excess moisture and also to preserve the meat from spoiling, and then hung to dry for seven to nine months. The fine, dry texture and flavour of the finished ham is superb. Ardennes ham – is also produced in Belgium, where it is brined, smoked and eaten within a month.

Protected Geographical Indication (PGI)

The Protected Geographical Indication is the name of an area or a specific place used as a description of an agricultural product or a foodstuff. The product must be produced in that area and thus have the characteristic properties attributable to that region.

Jambon de Bayonne has a wonderful rich, nutty flavour and is a famous speciality of the Pays Basque region in southwest France. Its origins date back to the twelfth century – medieval church carvings depict this celebrated ham, which was already a much sought-after luxury – and later, Henri IV had it delivered to him in Paris. Bayonne ham is displayed proudly by farmers and pork butchers at the annual *Foire au jambon*, the Easter fair that has been held in Bayonne every year since 1462. Stalls line the banks of the River Nive and *dégustations* (tastings) and demonstrations take part in the old part of the town.

The name 'Bayonne ham' is protected by a special registration process (the ham has the European PGI – Protected Geographical Indication status – see above right) and everyone involved in the production, from pig farmers to processors, formed a consortium to apply for this registration, which can be used only for genuine Bayonne hams. The regulations are very strict: the meat must come from one of eight clearly defined breeds of pig and their diet must be free from steroids, fish oils and antibiotics. In fact, the Basque pigs live happily in the mountain forests on a diet of grass, roots, chestnuts, acorns and beechnuts. Only local salt (from Salies-de-Béarn) can be used for salting the hams, along with saltpetre, sugar, pepper and herbs. The hams must also mature for a minimum of seven months, although many are matured for up to 10 months. The superb flavour of the ham is very much dependent on the quality of the salt, the local climate, the effects of the Atlantic Ocean and the southerly wind, or *foehn*, which imparts its own elusive touch. Some producers rub wine or a paste of Espelette peppers into the skin, thus imparting a beautiful tawny colour and distinctive flavour to the end product.

Once the ham has completed its curing process, it is marked with the traditional '*Croix Basque*' (Basque cross) topped with the name Bayonne. The finished hams will keep for up to a year if kept in a cool dry atmosphere.

This delicious ham is widely regarded as among the best air-dried hams in the world. The firm-textured, dark red meat is interspersed with specks of tasty fat and just melts in the mouth. It is best sliced thinly and served at room temperature, alone or with Charentais melon or figs, or used in the many Basque dishes calling for ham.

Jambon de Vendée is a raw, boneless ham, dry-salted with sea salt and slightly dried; it is flavoured with eau de vie and aromatic herbs, which give it a wonderful flavour. It is usually cooked before eating.

The pretty town of Luxeuil-les-Bains, in the Haute-Saône region in the mountains of Franche-Comté in eastern France, is famous for its health-giving thermal springs and beautiful lace, and is also renowned for its magnificent hams known as *Jambon de Luxeuil*. Luxeuil hams graced the tables of discerning nobles in Rome two thousand years ago. Made from local pigs, the ham has a unique flavour that comes from the curing and smoking process. The hams are marinated in a mixture of red Jura wine, herbs and spices for four weeks and then dry salt is rubbed in by hand. They are kept in a cool, dry place for four weeks and then washed, after which they are smoked over conifer or cherry wood before maturing for 5–8 months in drying chambers. The cold, dry climate of the region provides the perfect conditions needed for drying the hams. Beware of imitations – to be sure a ham is authentic, look for the regional Franche-Comté Seal of Quality emblem, which will appear on the label or the seal. The hams have a golden brown rind and the meat is very tender, with a slightly salty, subtly smoky, spicy flavour.

Germany

Ham (*schinken*), both raw and cooked, is popular in Germany, with a wealth of regional variations that differ according to the ingredients added during the curing process (such as caraway seeds, coriander and juniper berries), and also the type of wood (beech, juniper or pine) used to smoke the ham. Hams are categorised as *Kochenschinken* (ham on the bone), *Nussschinken* (fillet ham), *Rollschinken* (rolled ham) and *Schinkenspeck* (fatty ham), according to the way in which the ham is cut, spiced, smoked, dried or stored.

Schwarzwälder Schinken (Black Forest ham) is probably the most famous German ham, which comes from Baden-Württemberg in the southwest of the country. This distinctive, dry-cured ham has a characteristic deep-red colour and intense smoky flavour. The ham is made from the knuckle of the rear leg of the pig, which is boned, cured with salt and spices, then smoked and aged for six to nine months. It was traditionally coated with beef blood, which gave it a black surface, but now, the blackened exterior is more commonly the result of the spices applied and the smoking process.

The raw meat is salted and seasoned with spices such as coriander, pepper, elderberries and juniper berries and left for two weeks; the salt is removed and the ham is left for another two weeks and then cold-smoked over fir or pine wood at a temperature of 25°C/77°F for several weeks, during which time the ham acquires its deep-red colour and much of its flavour. It is then aged for a minimum of six months.

Protected Designation of Origin (PDO)

The Protected Designation of Origin is the name of an area or a particular place, used as a designation for an agricultural product or a foodstuff. The product must come from the area or place whose quality or geographical environment notably or exclusively determines its properties. The production, processing and preparation must also take place within the determined geographical area.

Production of the ham is controlled by strict regulations that determine where the ham can be produced and the precise curing and ageing processes. The moist climate of the Black Forest region is ideally suited to air-drying the ham, resulting in full-bodied flavoursome meat with a dense texture. The term 'Black Forest ham' is a Protected Designation of Origin (PDO) product in the European Union, meaning that anything sold in the EU as 'Black Forest ham' must come from the Black Forest and be made in accordance with the regulations.

Westfälischer Schinken (Westphalian ham) is a regional speciality from northern Germany, the 'home of ham', as the region calls itself. Westphalian ham is made from hind leg of pork, which is first dry-salted, then brined, washed with clean water to reduce the saltiness and then smoked over aromatic wood. Renowned for its wonderful flavour and tender texture, it has been considered a delicacy in Westphalia for centuries – it was popular with the ancient Romans – and is very popular throughout Germany and the rest of the world. Westphalian hams were fashionable in England for a time. Samuel Pepys mentioned the ham in his famous *Diary* in 1661 '…and then with my aunt Wight, my wife, and Pall and I to her house by coach, and there staid and supped upon a Westphalia ham, and so home and to bed.'

This ham comes from pigs fed on vegetables, clover, stinging nettles, acorns and beech mast (although excessive consumption of the latter is discouraged because it makes the pigs sluggish). Traditionally made hams are smoked slowly over beechwood and juniper. This combination of a gourmet diet, curing and smoking results in a dark brown, very dense ham with a unique, light smoky flavour.

Other German hams include: *Ammerländer Schinken*, a cured ham that has been cold-smoked over beechwood and juniper berries; *Katenspeck*, a cured, smoked and cooked ham (*Katen* means 'barn' in German, indicating that this ham is made 'farmhouse-style'); and *Landrauch*, a 'country smoked' ham, which is heavily smoked and has a dry texture.

Italy

In Italy, ham is called *prosciutto*, and can be either cooked (*prosciutto cotto*) or raw dry-cured (*prosciutto crudo*). The latter has been made in Italy since antiquity, the name coming from the Latin word '*perexuctus*', which translates as 'deprived of all liquid'. Although the principles of making a *prosciutto* are the same, each region has its own specific standards, which must be met in order for the ham to be designated as a Protected Designation of Origin (PDO, see page 115) *prosciutto*. Regional consortiums maintain the integrity of *prosciutto*, protect trade secrets and ensure that the strict rules are followed. Each consortium has its own specific brand or trademark which should be visible on the ham.

To make *prosciutto*, pork thighs are first hung in well-ventilated or refrigerated rooms for 24–36 hours. The fat and hide is then trimmed and the salt-curing process begins. *Prosciutto*-makers massage and apply salt to the meat, repeating the procedure once a week for a month. *Prosciutto* is sometimes cured with saltpetre (either sodium or potassium nitrite), which inhibits the growth of bacteria and produces a pink colour and unique flavour. The hams are then washed, brushed and dried, either in sunlight or indoors, where temperatures never exceed 15°C/59°F. After several months, they are beaten with wooden bats into the traditional round and flattened shape. Areas of muscle tissue not covered by skin are coated with a mixture of ground-up fat, flour, salt and pepper to form in time a kind of 'seal' that will keep the meat moist and fresh. The next stage is the ageing period in cool rooms, which varies according to the type of ham. During this long ageing period, hams will lose up to a third of their weight. Some of the best-known *prosciutto* varieties include:

Prosciutto di Parma (Parma ham) is a large raw ham with a sweet flavour and creamy texture. *Prosciutto di Parma* is produced in the Emilia-Romagna region and is Italy's most popular and well-known ham; it is also widely exported. Its origins date back to at least the first century BC; Cato, a Roman author, praised the quality of the region's hams. The excellence of the ham was largely due to the favourable climate and the abundance of pastures and pig-friendly scrublands.

Parma ham is made from large, locally raised pigs that are fed a strictly controlled diet which includes whey from locally made Parmigiano-Reggiano cheese. The curing process, done by a *maestri salatori* (master salter), uses comparatively little salt, but can also include garlic and sugar, which produce sweeter meat. After salting, the meat is sealed with pig fat, which slows drying. The curing process takes at least 12 months and up to two years and is supervised by a *maestro prosciuttaio* (ham master), who probes the inside muscle of the ham with a long stick and can tell just by smelling the stick how the ham is developing and if it is ready. The best of these exceptional hams is said to come from the village of Langhirano, just south of the city of Parma.

The rose-pink meat is firm and dense with a sweet flavour – connoisseurs say that the meat nearest the bone has the most flavour. There is a saying in Parma: *'Grasso e magro non del tutto, ecco il pregio del prosciutto'*, which means the ham must have the correct ratio of fat and lean meat (and note the value of the prosciutto). It is usually thinly sliced and eaten raw (often with melon) but can be used in cooking. Italians use the rind to flavour soups. Production is controlled by the local producers' association, the *Consorzio del Prosciutto di Parma*, which safeguards the quality of Parma prosciutto and guarantees that the ham is locally cured and dried in the time-honoured way. A genuine Parma ham will bear the mark of a five-pointed ducal crown, symbol of the *Consorzio*.

Prosciutto di San Daniele is a highly prized ham that has been made for hundreds of years in Friuli Venezia-Giulia, a region in northeastern Italy between the Alps and the Adriatic. The dry air and high altitudes of the region give the ham its wonderful velvety texture and sweet-salty flavour. Its distinguishing feature is that it is cured with the bottom part of the leg bone in. The hams are cured with local sea salt and must be aged for at least 12 months, but some are aged for up to two years. It is delicious eaten with country bread and a soft, sweet cheese such as Taleggio or Montasio. Its salty flavour is offset by sweet fruits such as melon or figs.

Prosciutto Crudo Toscano is the Tuscan version of *prosciutto*. It is made from pigs reared and slaughtered in Tuscany and cured with sea salt, pepper and aromatic herbs such as garlic, juniper or rosemary, which result in a unique flavour, imbued with the inimitable bouquet of Tuscany.

Culatello is an artisainal delicacy in Emilia-Romagna is rarely seen outside Italy, or indeed outside the Emilia-Romagna region. It is made from meat high up on the right hind leg and has less fat than other *prosciutti*. An expensive and very tender high-quality cut, it is cured with salt, pepper, garlic and dry wine, then sewn inside a pig's bladder, tied tightly to expel air, and air-dried for a long time – usually for 400 days. The rosy red meat has a rich, yet delicate, almost sweet flavour and a melting, creamy texture. Some hams are cured and soaked in wine to add even more flavour. Delicious *culatello* has a revered place in Italian cuisine. Bonaventura Angeli, in his *Historia della città di Parma*, refers to *culatello* being served in 1322 at the wedding of Count Andrea Rossi and Giovanna di San Vitale. *Culatello di Zibello* (made in Zibello, near Modena) has PDO status (see page 115).

Speck is a smoked, salt-cured, air-dried ham with a distinctive taste, produced on the Austrian/Italian borders. It is delicious on its own and can be added to stews and soups to add flavour.

Spain

Spain is passionate about *jamón* (ham). The earliest written reference to Spanish hams was from the historian Strabo in the first century BC, who praised them in *Geographica*.

The numerous food shops and bars found in every city and town offer a wonderful variety of tasty hams. The *Museo del Jamón* restaurants in Madrid are a Spanish institution and eating in them is treated almost as a religious experience. An enormous range of hams from all over Spain, hangs from the ceilings; they are available to buy and take away as well as to order in the restaurants.

The province of Extremadura, bordering Portugal, is the heart of pig country. Montánchez, a village in the province, is particularly renowned throughout Spain for its exquisite ham; Monesterio, another town in the province, hosts an annual ham festival in September, while ham producers in several other towns in the region, such as Calera de León and Cabeza la Vaca, display images of happy, smiling pigs.

Of the many types of Spanish ham, probably the most celebrated is the famous *Jamón Ibérico*. From southwest Spain, this is an artisan ham that the Spanish claim as the best ham in the world and which is much in demand by connoisseurs.

This exceptional ham was enjoyed in antiquity, when the ancient Greeks praised its fine flavour and texture, and it is still made in the age-old way, from the hind legs of native, dark-coloured pigs. Known as *pata negra*, or 'black feet', they are descendants of the region's wild boar and they roam freely in the *dehesa* (Spanish oak-forest), where they forage for acorns, chestnuts, fungi and aromatic plants. Acorns that are out of reach are shaken free from high branches by a *varreadore*, a man using a *varra* (a long stick with a leather cord attached). Ibérico pigs get plenty of exercise, which causes the fat to be marbled throughout the meat.

The freshly cut hind legs are salted for up to 10 days, then washed and left to 'rest' for up to two months in cold, humid rooms to allow the meat to dry out. This period is known as the *asentamiento*, a slow process during which the ham loses water and the salt is absorbed and spread through every part of the ham. The hams are then moved to a *secadero* (natural drying area, where temperature and humidity are controlled through ventilation) and left for 6–9 months. The hams lose moisture as they mature and it is during this phase that they begin to develop their flavour, aroma and deep-red colour. The hams are regularly inspected by a skilled *calador* (ham master), who decides when the hams should be moved to the *bodega* (cellar or curing house) to finish curing and reach their optimum flavour. The hams are dry-cured for a minimum of two years and up to 30 months in the cold, dry mountain air, although some hams are aged even longer (the additional curing is called *añejado*). Longer ageing produces hams with a very distinctive and even richer, more complex flavour. Like fine wines, *Ibérico* ham has different 'vintages' influenced by many factors – for instance, the quality of the acorns the pigs ate, the climate, and the conditions in which the hams are matured. The smooth, almost silky, deep-red meat is nicely flecked with fat and has a distinctive fragrance and an intense, complex, slightly nutty flavour with a lingering sweet-salty tang, which complements the highly aromatic fat.

Jamón Ibérico de Bellota is a choice ham (*bellota* means acorn) from the same breed of pig and is cured by the same methods, but the pigs are fed solely on acorns from about the age of 15 months, when they weigh about 90 kg (198 lb), until they reach their slaughter weight of around 160–190 kg (352–418 lb). The period in the autumn when the acorns fall is called the '*montanera*' and during this time (about three months) each pig will eat roughly 9 kg (20 lb) of acorns a day. While most *Jamón Ibérico* is cured for around two years, *Jamón Ibérico de Bellota* is cured for about three years, and some 'reserve' hams are cured for more than four years. Due to the pigs' natural diet of mainly acorns, at least half the fat content is the same form as that of olive oil, which is well known for improving or maintaining good cholesterol levels.

Paletilla Ibérico de Bellota undergoes the same processes as above, but the meat is not from the hind leg of the pig, but from the shoulder or front leg and is smaller with more fat. Nevertheless, *paletilla* is very tasty and is less expensive than *Jamón Ibérico de Bellota*.

Above: An Ibérico pig.

Other Ibérico hams include: *Jamón Ibérico de Recebo*, from Iberian pigs that have been fed on cereals (a maximum of 30 per cent) and acorns during the final fattening process; and *Jamón Ibérico de Pienso*, or simply *Jamón Ibérico*, from Iberian pigs that have been fattened solely on grain. Hams such as *Dehesa de Extremadura* (from areas in Cáceres province and south of Badajoz) and *Jamón de Huelva* (produced in the Sierra de Huelva and Guijuelo-Salamanca from Castile and León) are also made from the same breed of pig and have been given PDO (Protected Designation of Origin, see page 115) status.

The Real Ibérico Consortium for the Promotion of Spanish Ibérico Cured Ham is an independent, non-profit making association that has united the top companies from all the traditional Iberian ham-producing regions since 1996. Its key function is to maximise international awareness of Iberian ham as one of the best gourmet products on the market and to guarantee the quality of Iberian hams that are sold outside Spain by the use of the *'Real Ibérico'* brand stamp.

Jamón Ibérico is delicious accompanied by a glass of red wine or dry sherry. Put it in your mouth and savour it slowly as its melts on your tongue. Sometimes tiny white crystals occur in the meat; these are crystals of the amino acid tyrosine and are completely harmless and safe to eat; indeed, connoisseurs regard them as a guarantee of the authenticity of the ham.

Jamón Serrano is a dry-cured ham that takes its name from the mountainous areas (*sierra*) throughout Spain. Leaner, larger and paler than Ibérico hams, *Jamón Serrano* is made from the hind legs of white domesticated pigs. Since time immemorial, the pigs were slaughtered around 11 November, St Martin's Day, when the weather conditions were most suited to curing the hams. The hams were rolled in sea salt on a table called the *saladero* and left for several weeks. After the salt was washed off, the hams were hung to dry from the rafters in the dry, cold air of the region, or in *secaderos* (rooms with large shuttered windows that allowed the air flow to be controlled), and 12–18 months later the hams had slowly developed their characteristic flavour and aroma.

Today, the hams are still cured with sea salt, but modern technology allows the temperature, humidity and air flow to be controlled more efficiently. However, whenever climatic conditions are suitable this automatically switches off and nature takes over. After salting, the hams are washed and left to stand, allowing one day per kilo, during which time the salt penetrates the meat and moisture is drawn out. Next, the hams are hung on racks for up to 60 days. The next phase involves raising the temperature slowly, to replicate the climate and humidity in spring and summer and it is during this phase that the fat slowly impregnates the muscle tissue and the meat develops its distinctive texture, flavour and aroma. Serrano hams are hung for a minimum of nine months, but most are hung for up to 14 months or sometimes longer. The meat is firm with a slightly nutty aroma and intense flavour with a hint of sweetness and a lingering aftertaste.

The '*Jamón Serrano*' name is protected under EU regulations as a Traditional Speciality Guaranteed (TSG); this term does not impose any restrictions on the geographical origin of the product. *Serrano Consorcio* is a term that designates a serrano ham of a quality stipulated and guaranteed by the Spanish Serrano Ham Consortium (*Consorcio del*

Traditional Speciality Guaranteed (TSG)

The Traditional Speciality Guaranteed is a trademark for a product with particular characteristics that set it apart from other similar products in the same category. Although the product does not have to be manufactured in a specific geographically defined area, it must be manufactured using traditional ingredients or must be characteristic for its traditional composition, production process, or a processing that uses traditional methods.

Jamón Español). The most important specification is the minimum curing period of 36 weeks. *Jamón Serrano* from the consortium has a label with an 'S' in the shape of a ham, and says *Serrano Español*.

Jamón de Teruel is a serrano ham made in the Teruel province in Aragón, and has Spain's oldest PDO (Protected Designation of Origin, see page 115) status for cured ham. The ham must be made from local pigs that are at least eight months old and which have been fed on milk for 1½ months and barley for the remaining 6½ months. The pigs are butchered when they reach a weight between 115–130 kg (253–286 lb). The ham is cured for at least 12 months in natural conditions and is produced in small quantities only. PDO Teruel hams are branded with an eight-pointed star.

The *Feria del jamón de Teruel* (Teruel Ham Fair) is a wonderful gastronomic event, with workshops, tastings, competitions and other events. It takes place in during the month of September.

Jamón Serrano Trevélez is a high-quality *jamón serrano* produced in Trevélez, the highest village in Spain, situated on the southern slopes of the Sierra Nevada in Granada province in Andalucia. This superb ham can be matured for up to two years and has an excellent reputation for its fine flavour and texture, so much so that the ham has been given PGI status (Protected Geographical Indication, see page 113).

To enjoy all these exquisite Spanish hams at their best, it is essential that they are cut correctly by an expert. A skilled slicer will get the very best out of the ham by cutting wafer-thin slices in a way that exposes part of the ham to the air, thus ensuring that the flavour and aroma develop fully.

THE RECIPES

to cook a ham in comfort

This idea came from a book belonging to my mother, called *Food in England* by Dorothy Hartley. As a child, I used to love flicking through the pages and looking at the very simple pen and ink drawings by an unacknowledged artist. The one that accompanies this recipe shows a huge pot with its side removed so we can see the ham nestled on a bed of vegetables – very comfortable it looks too! Several of the recipes that follow use cooked ham, so if you happen to find yourself with leftovers...

1 x 3–4 kg/6½ lb–8½ lb green (unsmoked) gammon
2 leeks, trimmed, roughly chopped (include the green part) and washed
2 large onions, cut in two with the skins on
4 carrots, peeled and roughly chopped
2 sticks of celery, roughly chopped

any tops of vegetables or peelings of parsnips, turnips, and so on
1 bunch of parsley
1 sprig of thyme
6 cloves
a few peppercorns
2 cooking apples and any peelings
250 g/9 oz black treacle
1 x 500 ml/18 fl oz bottle of ale (any type)

You need to start this the day before. Soak the gammon for 24 hours to remove the salt, changing the water once.

Place the vegetables, apples, peelings (if you have them), herbs and spices in a large cooking pot. Drain the ham and add to the pot, then add the apples, pour in the treacle and ale and top up with water to just cover. Bring to the boil and simmer, uncovered, for 4–5 hours.

Remove from the heat and leave to cool in the liquid. When it is completely cold, lift out the ham and trim off excess fat. Will keep for about 2 weeks in the fridge.

leek and ham with cheese sauce

This is a great supper dish and ideal for leftover bits of ham; you can even add small amounts of cured ham or, dare I say it, any dried edges from the expensive sorts of Italian or French cured hams. They will add a great depth of flavour.

SERVES 4

2 leeks, trimmed
500 g/1 lb 2oz cooked
  ham, cut into 2 cm/
  ³/₄ inch cubes
60 g/2¹/₂ oz butter
60 g/2¹/₂ oz plain flour
600 ml/1 pint hot milk
2 tsp Dijon mustard
100 g/3¹/₂ oz mature
  cheddar or Gruyère
  cheese, grated
salt and pepper

Preheat the oven to 200°C/400°F/gas 6.

Slice and wash the leeks. Blanch for 2 minutes in a pan of boiling salted water, then drain and refresh in cold water. Set aside to drain thoroughly.

Mix the leeks with the ham and place in a large ovenproof dish, leaving room to pour the sauce on top.

Melt the butter in a pan, then stir in the flour and cook, stirring, for a few minutes. Slowly add the milk, whisking constantly, to create a smooth but thickish sauce – don't add all the milk if it seems to be getting thin. Remove from the heat and mix in the mustard and half the cheese and check for seasoning. Pour over the ham and leek mixture, sprinkle on the rest of the cheese and bake in the oven for about 30 minutes, until browned and bubbling.

ham and haddie

This recipe exemplifies the tradition of combinations of simple ingredients producing something greater than the sum of the parts. Smoking food began simply as a way of preserving foods. Originally, smoked ham was used in this dish, but I think, with the smoked haddock, it tends to be over-rich, especially with the cream. I prefer to use a slice of unsmoked cooked ham and it is perfect as a light supper dish.

SERVES 4

4 small, undyed smoked
  haddock
2 tsp butter
4 slices of ham
5 tbsp double cream
black pepper

Preheat the grill. Poach the haddock in a little simmering water for about 4 minutes, transfer to a serving dish and keep warm, but don't allow to dry out. Put the poaching liquid to one side.

Heat the butter in a frying pan and gently warm the ham through. Place a slice of ham on top of each fish.

Pour the water used for poaching the haddock into the pan used for the ham, then add the cream, season with black pepper and simmer gently until thickened slightly. Pour this sauce over the ham and haddock and put under the hot grill briefly. Serve immediately.

ham, chicken and mushroom pie

Ham and chicken go well together and this pie mix can be added to with herbs or cooked vegetables. It's a great party dish since it looks very impressive and all the work is done in advance, leaving you to enjoy yourself!

SERVES 6–8

FOR THE PASTRY
150 g/5 oz chilled butter,
  cut into cubes
300 g/11 oz plain flour,
  plus extra for dusting
1/2 tsp salt
75 ml/2 1/2 fl oz ice-cold water
1 small egg, beaten, to glaze

FOR THE FILLING
3 tbsp olive oil
500 g/1 lb 2 oz raw chicken, diced
1 onion, peeled and chopped
2 sticks of celery, finely diced
2 carrots, peeled and finely diced
115 g/4 oz button mushrooms, sliced
2 garlic cloves, peeled and crushed
350 g/12 oz cooked ham, diced
salt and pepper

FOR THE SAUCE
50 g/2 oz butter
50 g/2 oz plain flour
450 ml/3/4 pint hot chicken stock
100 ml/3 1/2 fl oz milk
75 ml/2 1/2 fl oz double cream
2 tbsp chopped fresh flat-leaf parsley

Make the pastry in a food processor: whiz the butter, flour and salt to form breadcrumbs, then pour on just enough cold water until a dough begins to form, but don't allow it to form a ball – this way, you keep the butter in tiny lumps and not a paste. Work the pastry lightly into a ball by hand, cover and set aside for 30 minutes to rest.

To make the filling, heat 2 tbsp olive oil in a pan. Season the chicken and quickly brown in the pan for about 8 minutes, then set aside. Add more oil to the pan if necessary, and fry the onion, celery, carrots and mushrooms until softened. Add the garlic and cook gently for a further 3 minutes, then set aside. Preheat the oven to 190°C/375°F/gas 5.

To make the sauce, melt the butter in a large saucepan and stir in the flour, then cook, stirring, for a few minutes. Gradually pour in the hot stock and bring to the boil, whisking, then add the milk and cream. Allow to simmer for 5 minutes, then season with salt and pepper and add the parsley.

Mix the ham with the chicken and vegetables, then pour the sauce in and mix well. Place in a 1.5 litre/2½ pint pie dish.

Roll out the pastry on a lightly floured surface to a good 2 cm/¾ inch wider than the dish. Brush the edges of the pie dish with beaten egg, then place the pastry on top, pressing it down to stick, and create a neat edge. Brush with more egg, then cook in the oven for about 50 minutes, until brown.

feijoada

This dish originated in Brazil as a sort of workers' stew, rather like the French cassoulet, in which beans and meats are cooked together. The traditional dish used all sorts of pig parts, from the ears to the feet, but this version is a little simpler. If you have a Portuguese delicatessen near you, they may sell salted ribs, which should be soaked overnight, along with the beans. Otherwise, use fresh ribs.

SERVES 6–8

500 g/1 lb 2 oz dried
  black beans
1 smoked ham hock,
  about 1.3 kg/3 lb
6–8 pork ribs
1 pig's trotter, split
  and rinsed
2 large garlic cloves,
  peeled and chopped
4 bay leaves
400 g/14 oz cured garlic
  sausage, cut into chunks
4 small, juicy oranges,
  peeled and sliced

You need to start this the day before. Rinse the beans, cover with cold water and soak overnight. Soak the ham hock in cold water overnight.

When ready to cook, rinse the beans and place in a large casserole with the ham hock, ribs, trotter, garlic and bay leaves. Cover with water and bring to the boil, skimming off any scum. Reduce the heat and simmer gently, uncovered, for 2½ hours, skimming occasionally. Take out a ladleful of beans and mash them with a fork, then return to the pan, adding the garlic sausage and simmer for a further 30 minutes.

To serve, place the orange slices on top and spoon the feijoada straight from the pot, accompanied with fluffy steamed rice.

tomato, ham and herb tarts

I keep a supply of pastry bases in the deep freeze for those emergency occasions
when you need a first course. You can simply chop up a few tomatoes, sprinkle
with some bacon or roast peppers, or olives maybe, and slide them into a hot oven
– lo and behold, a delicious individual crisp tart. The ham in this recipe can be
replaced with prosciutto or bacon. Herbs also can be added – whatever you have
to hand: wild garlic is good in season.

MAKES 4 TARTS

flour for dusting
300 g/11 oz puff pastry
150 g/5 oz cooked ham
2 tbsp virgin olive oil
20 cherry tomatoes, halved
2 garlic cloves, peeled
  and sliced
2 tsp chopped fresh
  basil or thyme
black pepper

Preheat the oven to 190°C/375°F/gas 5.

On a lightly floured surface, roll out the pastry – not too thinly, as you
want it to rise with some texture. Cut it into 4 discs of about 15 cm/
6 inch diameter. Using a small saucer or dish as a guide, make a light
incision about 1 cm/½ inch in from the edge all the way around. Leave
to rest in the fridge (or freezer) until you need them.

Roughly shred the ham and mix with a little of the olive oil.

Put the cherry tomatoes and garlic into a bowl and mix with a little more
olive oil, the herbs and black pepper. Spoon the ham onto the base of the
tarts and spread out, keeping within the 1 cm/½ inch circle, then spoon
on the tomatoes. Cook in the oven for about 15 minutes until the pastry
is golden and crisp. Allow to rest for a few minutes, then serve with a splash
of olive oil.

ham with asparagus and Hollandaise

This is one of those delicious dishes that is very good as a first course or for supper. On no account use tinned asparagus, as you need the texture of fresh asparagus. The British green asparagus or French and German white asparagus are equally good.

SERVES 4

20 asparagus spears, trimmed to the same length as the ham
4 large slices of ham

FOR THE HOLLANDAISE SAUCE
200 g/7 oz unsalted butter, melted
2 egg yolks
1 tbsp dry white wine
juice of ½ lemon
salt and black pepper

Make the sauce first, as this can be kept warm. The melted butter must not be too hot, or it will scramble the eggs.

In a stainless steel pan, whisk together the egg yolks and wine over a low heat until they thicken slightly, taking the pan on and off the heat as you whisk so that you don't overcook the eggs. They are ready when the mixture leaves its trail when the whisk is lifted.

Take off the heat and place the pan on a work surface with a damp cloth underneath it to stop it moving about. While continuously whisking, slowly pour the melted butter onto the mixture until it has all been incorporated and the sauce is thick. Season with the lemon juice and salt and pepper to taste, then set aside in a warm place.

Plunge the asparagus into a pan of boiling salted water and cook for about 7 minutes – you should then be able to slide a sharp knife through the asparagus 1 cm/½ inch below the green tip. Remove and drain well.

Place five asparagus spears on each of four warmed plates, place the ham on top, then spoon on generous amounts of sauce. You can brown briefly under a hot grill if you like, but this is not necessary.

pease pudding

'Pease pudding hot, pease pudding cold
Pease pudding in the pot, nine days old
Some like it hot, some like it cold
Some like it in the pot, nine days old.'

This old nursery rhyme celebrates one of the oldest dishes in the English repertoire. Traditionally, it was made with old mealy peas and then served with boiled bacon or ham. The peas, once soaked overnight, were seasoned with mint and perhaps a little sugar, then tied up in a greased pudding cloth and suspended in a pan in which a ham or bacon piece was cooking, such as the 'to cook a ham in comfort' (see page 126). This version, from Elisabeth Luard's wonderful book, *European Peasant Cookery*, is very good served with sausages or roast pork.

SERVES 6–8

500 g/1 lb 2oz dried
  or split peas
water or ham stock (if you
  have a ham bone to add
  to the water, so much the
  better)
1 small bunch of fresh mint
50 g/2 oz butter
salt and ground black
  pepper

Soak the dried peas in cold water for several hours or overnight. Drain and place in a pan and cover with the water or stock. Add the mint and black pepper and salt, if you are using water, and cook gently until soft, for about 1 hour.

Preheat the oven to 160°C/325°F/ gas 3. Drain the liquid off and remove the mint, then mash the peas with the butter, seasoning to taste. Place the mixture in a pudding bowl and cover with buttered foil. Place in a bain marie (see page 274) and cook in the oven for 1 hour. As the rhyme suggests, it can be reheated.

pea and ham soup

Versions of this dish are found in peasant cookery throughout northern Europe; it was a mainstay in Scottish homes until well into the twentieth century. The use of dairy produce as a finishing touch is optional. Take care with salt — you may not need any extra because the ham bone may provide enough.

SERVES 6–8

225 g/8 oz dried yellow
  peas
2 potatoes
1 carrot
2.5 litres/4¼ pints ham
  stock or cold water
1 ham bone
fresh bouquet garni
  (see page 274)
225 g/8 oz smoked cured
  sausage, sliced
3 tbsp double cream
  or butter
salt and pepper

You need to start this the night before. Rinse the peas and soak in cold water overnight.

The next day, peel the potatoes and carrot and chop into rough dice. Drain the peas and place in a pan with the stock or water and the ham bone. Add the bouquet garni and pepper to taste and bring to the boil, skimming off any scum. Allow to simmer for 1½ hours.

Remove the ham bone, allowing any bits of ham adhering to it to slide off into the soup, and the bouquet garni. Cool a little, then liquidise and return to the pan. Add the sliced sausage and simmer for another 15 minutes.

Check for seasoning. Serve in hot bowls with a swirl of cream or, more traditionally, a knob of butter.

HAM SANDWICH WITH HONEY, MUSTARD & LAMBS LETTUCE

Cold ham is a delight and served as a salad is great with pickles or Mostarda, but you can carry the condiment idea through in a sandwich as well. Try slices of ham with lambs lettuce, make sure it's well washed as the tiny roots can often have sandy soil adhering to them. Smear the bread (probably a brown, textured, variety) with a honey mustard then lots of the lambs lettuce and a thick slice of ham, no salt or pepper is usually needed as the lambs lettuce provides the heat and the ham the salt.

HAM BAGUETTE WITH BRIE & TOMATO

Cold cooked ham is also delicious in a baguette, the crunchy texture of the crust is softened with the brie and tomatoes. Take a medium-sized baguette (or cut a piece from a longer one) and slice open leaving one side as a sort of hinge, horizontally. Spread with a mild or honey mustard then add 4 slices of tomato, season with a little sea salt and olive oil. Place two long thin strips of brie down the middle. It doesn't have to fill the space, unless you want it to of course. Add some sliced ham and eat!

THE HAM SANDWICH

Ham makes for a delicious sandwich filling and can be accompanied with infinite other flavours and fillings. Here are three of my favourites: always remember you can toast the bread or make ham and cheese toasties as a warm alternative.

CROISSANT SANDWICH WITH PROSCIUTTO & BLACK OLIVE PASTE

I love croissants as a sandwich base. Slice the croissant horizontally and spread a thin layer of olive paste on the base then fill with leaves of rocket. Next, curl in 4 thin slices of prosciutto and finish with a splash of olive oil.

SAUSAGES
BLOOD PU

in praise of the humble sausage

All around the world, people enjoy sausages in an enormous variety of shapes and sizes, with countless different flavourings and seasonings. After the killing of a pig, sausages were originally made as a means of preserving the edible bits and pieces left over after the carcass had been jointed. They were either eaten fresh or were air-dried or smoked to preserve for future use. The word 'sausage' comes from the Latin word *salsus*, which means salted or preserved. At its most basic, a sausage is a mixture of chopped meats, seasonings and flavourings stuffed into a casing (originally this would have been the animal's intestines, and these are still widely used as natural casings). The diversity of the many hundreds of mouth-watering sausages is due to the well-judged and thoughtful use of seasonings and skilful curing techniques by craft butchers and *charcutiers* over the centuries.

The Sumerians (from modern-day Iraq) were making sausages 5000 years ago and in ancient Greece and Rome, several types of sausages were sold hot from street stalls. Sausage-sellers also sold their wares to the audiences enjoying performances in the theatres of ancient Greece. The Romans introduced sausages, both smoked and unsmoked, to all the countries of their Empire, where they gradually took on distinctive national characteristics.

The three main categories of sausage are: fresh raw sausages, which need cooking; cooked or partly cooked sausages, such as saveloy and frankfurter, which may be eaten hot or cold; and cured sausages, such as salami, which are air-dried and/or smoked and are usually sliced and eaten cold.

When buying fresh sausages, look for plump sausages with a high meat content (70 per cent or more) and natural skins. Top-quality sausages use natural casings, which are slightly porous and allow the sausage to cook without bursting. Artificial casings, made from collagen or cellulose, tend to be tough and inclined to stick to the pan if the sausages are fried. Never prick sausages – they should be cooked slowly (to ensure that the skins do not burst) until cooked through, but still juicy.

Cured sausages are in Mediterranean countries, where the warm, dry climate allows sausages and other meats to be air-dried. Cured sausages are preserved by mixing the raw chopped meat with salt, saltpetre, spices and sometimes alcohol. The mixture is packed into casings and dried for a period of time. Saltpetre inhibits the growth of many harmful bacteria, and the spices also help to preserve the meat. During the drying period, the cured sausage will undergo fermentation by bacteria that produce lactic acid and impart a pleasantly acid flavour to the sausage. As the sausage dries, it shrinks and can lose up to half its original weight. When completely dried, the sausage will keep for a long time. Cured sausages may also be smoked, which further inhibits bacterial growth.

THE DIFFERENT VARIETIES OF SAUSAGE

Sausages remain enormously popular throughout Europe, ranging from long-established traditional varieties to new and even more innovative flavour combinations.

Britain

The ancient Romans are thought to have introduced sausages to Britain: they were very fond of highly spiced and seasoned sausages, which provided a nutritious, portable food for the marching legions and were ideal for using up bits and pieces left over from the pig's carcass. The conquering Normans introduced their own sausages and they too quickly became established throughout Britain. Sausages and black puddings were sold in medieval cookshops in England's towns, and Henry V declared that 'War without fire is as worthless as sausages without mustard.'

New developments in sausage-making occurred in the seventeenth century, when sausages were divided into links and the skinless sausage was introduced. The latter was a godsend, as it meant there was no need to go to the trouble of cleaning and filling guts. Sausage meat was also packed into pots, ready for the cook to make as many sausages as were needed.

Nowadays, there are countless sausage varieties throughout Britain. One of the most celebrated is the Cumberland sausage: chunky, coarse-cut sausage spiced with black pepper, it is traditionally made in a continuous spiral and is sold by length rather than weight. Other popular British sausages include Lincolnshire, traditionally made with pork, bread and sage, although thyme is sometimes used instead; Gloucester, traditionally made with meat from Gloucester Old Spot pigs and flavoured with sage; Lorne, a Scottish, smooth-textured, square slicing sausage, made with beef and pork; Oxford, made with pork and veal and seasoned with lemon, sage, savory and marjoram; and Suffolk, a coarse sausage seasoned with herbs, similar to Lincolnshire.

Sausages made with organic and rare breed meats are particularly tasty and are increasing in popularity. Recently, enterprising manufacturers and butchers have created a terrific variety of speciality sausages with tantalising flavours, such as pheasant and wild boar, pork and banana, and pork and Stilton, which have resulted in new gourmet-style dishes, with a little more sophistication than good old 'bangers and mash'.

Bright red saveloys, made from highly seasoned pork, are particularly popular in the south of England. Their name comes from the French word *cervelas*, or Italian *cervello*, which in turn comes from Latin *cerebellum*, meaning brain, although nowadays saveloys are not made with pigs' brains.

Polony is a cooked pork sausage with a scarlet casing and is usually sliced and eaten cold. The name is probably a corruption of Bologna, the Italian town, or it may be derived from 'Polonia', as it is similar to Polish sausage. Polony made from finely ground lean pork, fat and rusk was popular in England in the seventeenth century and has always been coloured red, variously at times with saltpetre, red wine or cochineal. It was usually seasoned with cloves, mace, nutmeg and caraway and sometimes sage and thyme too. Polony was smoked for a few days, then dried and kept for several months. Polony made in Bath was famous in the past, as was that from Sheffield in Yorkshire. Some butchers still make their own polony, which is far superior to large-scale, commercially made versions.

Sausages are used in some popular British dishes such as Toad in the Hole (sausages baked in batter in a baking dish), Sausage Rolls (sausagemeat wrapped in pastry, see page 184), and Scotch Eggs (hardboiled eggs wrapped in sausagemeat, coated with egg and breadcrumbs and deep-fried, see page 182). The latter aren't particularly Scottish – their name may come from the fact that they're wrapped in finely chopped meat, which in eighteenth-century England was described as 'scotcht'.

Tasty and versatile, sausages are enjoyed for breakfast, lunch, dinner and snacks, and sizzling sausages are an essential part of the Great British Breakfast, along with bacon and eggs. They are great favourites at barbecues too, but they don't cook well on the fierce heat – almost everyone has experienced sausages that are charred on the outside and raw inside! If you're cooking them for a barbecue, the trick is to poach them in boiling water first for 30 minutes and then barbecue them for 10 minutes or so, to brown them and add that special smoky barbecue flavour.

The British certainly love sausages – five million are consumed every day in the United Kingdom. They were one of the few foods to escape rationing during the Second World War; at that time they lived up to their nickname, 'bangers', because they contained so much water that they exploded when fried. Nowadays, there's a national sausage week as well as regional and national competitions to find the best sausages in Britain, culminating in the 'Champion of Champions' award for the supreme sausage.

France

Fresh sausages are known as *saucissses* or *saucissons*, whether cured or smoked. They are sold by *charcutiers* throughout France and there are many different regional sausages, some of which are especially renowned for their exceptional quality and flavour.

Artisan charcuterie in Lyon can be traced back to the fourteenth century. *Rosette de Lyon*, a classic dried French sausage, is made from carefully selected cuts of meat. It is cured with red wine and *quatre épices* (four spices, see page 274), then packed into the large intestine, which terminates at the part of the pig euphemistically called the 'rosette', hence its name. This coarse-textured, dry-cured sausage is probably the most prestigious cured sausage in France, due to its rich wine flavour.

Other mountainous regions of France are also renowned for their sausages. In the Cévennes mountains of southern France, wild boar sausages (*saucissons de sanglier*) are popular, as are sausages containing peppers, apples or chestnuts. *La rayolette* is a traditional Cévenol sausage: a mixture of fat and lean pork is salted and left for three days, then spices and a dash of alcohol are added and the sausage is shaped and dried for about two months. It is usually sold whole.

Lozère, a département within the Cévennes, has a long tradition of producing a mouth-watering variety of hams and sausages, which are cured to perfection in the cold, dry mountain air. *La saucisse sèche Lozérienne* is always made from pure pork in a natural casing, but every butcher has his own recipe and method. *La saucisse sèche Lozérienne* can be bought in a piece or ready-sliced. *La saucisse d'herbe Lozérienne* is another speciality and the only traditional recipe that combines leafy vegetables (usually a combination of chard, cabbage and dandelion leaves) and herbs with the pork, spices and seasonings. The proportions of meat to vegetables and herbs vary according to the butcher and some butchers also add potatoes to the ingredients. This sausage is delicious grilled, fried or in a casserole.

Picturesque Troyes, the ancient capital of the Champagne region, is famous for its A*ndouillettes*, small, fresh sausages made from pig's intestines, which are much imitated by other regions. They are usually grilled and served hot and are especially delicious served with apples sautéed in butter. Louis II enjoyed it after his coronation in Troyes in 877, and both Louis XIV and Napoleon also ate *andouillettes* while staying in the city. *The Association Amicale des Amateurs d'Andouillette Authentique* represents and promotes the tasty speciality throughout France.

Saucisse de Toulouse (Toulouse sausage) is a long, fresh sausage made with coarsely chopped pork and seasoned with pepper; some varieties also contain wine and garlic. For the French, it's a key ingredient of cassoulet (see page 248).

Saucisse de Morteau, also known as *Belle de Morteau*, comes from the little Jura town of Morteau in the mountainous Franche-Comté region of eastern France. It is produced using only pork from pigs fattened traditionally in the Franche-Comté. In addition, to be permitted to use the label '*Saucisse de Morteau*', the sausages must be smoked for at least 48 hours over conifer and juniper wood in traditional pyramid shaped chimneys, called *tuyés*. These sausages are guaranteed by PGI status (see page 113), which denotes their quality, origin and method of preparation as a regional French speciality. *Jésus*, a larger, fatter version of Morteau sausage, is believed to have got its name from its resemblance to a baby in swaddling clothes; it is traditionally served at the *Réveillon* celebration (the meal after Christmas midnight mass). Morteau is so well known for its sausages that it holds an annual summer festival to pay tribute to the town's most famous export. Residents parade through the town centre, and there's a regional produce market and plenty of opportunity to sample the celebrated sausages.

In Corsica, *figatelli*, smoked liver sausages that also contain other offal such as kidneys, are highly prized. They are often cooked over an open fire to allow the excess fat to run out.

The Auveryne region of central France is famous for its pork products: air-dried charcuterie and various terrines and pâtés. *Pounti* is a local delicacy that can be prepared in many different ways, depending on the cook (see page 192). It originated as a tasty way of using up leftovers. *Pounti* is best described as a terrine that's a cross between a meat loaf and a soufflé and incorporates chopped pork or bacon, eggs, milk, flour, onions or shallots, a green vegetable (usually Swiss chard or spinach), fresh herbs (chervil, tarragon, parsley) and prunes or raisins. Some cooks plump the prunes beforehand in warm, slightly sweetened tea, while others add slices of ham, stale bread or spices. The ingredients are mixed, well seasoned and then baked in a dish and cut into slices to serve. In spring, dandelion leaves and/or sorrel are sometimes added to the ingredients. When properly made and not too fatty, the unlikely combination of flavours in *pounti* is surprisingly delicious; the prunes add a slightly sweet, fruity note.

Rillettes (pronounced 'ree-yet'), are a specialty of the Loire Valley where they have been enjoyed for hundreds of years (see page 210). *Rillettes* are a type of pâté, usually made with pork. Like many other present-day French gourmet specialities, *rillettes* were originally a peasant dish and a way of preserving scraps of meat. The shredded meat was cooked slowly with fat, then potted and sealed under a layer of melted fat to protect it from the air; it would then keep for months in a cool place.

Mamers, a town in the Sarthe département, is regarded as the capital of rillettes and even boasts a brotherhood called the 'Chevaliers des Rillettes Sarthoises', who promote the local speciality in French-speaking Europe and organise an annual competition involving approximately 200 French and Belgian producers of rillettes.

Commercially made fresh rillettes can be stored for several weeks in the refrigerator providing the fatty seal is not broken. Rillettes are also sold in sterilised glass jars and these will keep for up to 1 year unopened. Rillettes are never served chilled – they must be at room temperature. Serve them like pâté, with toast or good French bread and a salad of bitter leaves to cut through their richness.

Germany

Wurst (sausages) are a staple of the German diet and the average German gets through a staggering 30 kg (66 lb) of sausages each year. Every region in Germany has developed its own delicious sausage specialities and there are over a thousand varieties, many of which have become famous and popular throughout Germany, and indeed all over the world.

German sausages in Germany are categorised as Brühwurst (scalded in hot water or steam, or parboiled sausage); Kochwurst (cooked sausage); and Rohwurst (raw sausage made from cured, air-dried or smoked meat), which are a speciality of northern Germany.

In Germany, 60 per cent of all sausages manufactured are Brühwurst. All scalded sausage varieties are fresh products and should be refrigerated and eaten as soon as possible. The best-known Brühwurst include Frankfurters, made with finely chopped lean pork, salt, bacon fat and spices and then smoked; Knackwurst, very similar to Frankfurters but shorter and plumper (their name comes from the fact that when they are heated they bend and the skin splits with a cracking sound); Bockwurst, very similar to Frankfurters but made from a mixture of finely chopped beef and pork and usually larger than frankfurters; Schinkenwurst, a Westphalian speciality, made from flaked rather than chopped ham and smoked over beechwood and juniper (by law, they must contain more than 50 per cent ham); Extrawurst (Fleischwurst), a juicy, fine-textured, flavoursome sausage, which may be pink to light brown in colour; Bierwurst (beer sausage), a pinkish-red, very fine-textured, oval sausage made from a mixture of finely chopped pork and beef and sometimes garlic. It has no beer in the recipe despite its name, which comes from the fact that this particular sausage goes well with beer. *Bierschinken* is studded with chunks of ham and pistachios.

Pale and delicately flavoured *Weisswurst* (white sausage) is a speciality of Munich and is made with veal, pork, cream and eggs. The story goes that it was created in Munich in 1857 by a young butcher, Sepp Moser, when he ran out of thick sausage skins. He filled some thin casings with meat, then boiled them for 10 minutes to make them firmer. His customers loved the tasty sausages and they have been a speciality there ever since.

Kochwurst are fully cooked and are not intended for keeping. *Liverwurst* (liver sausage) is a well-known cooked sausage that is available in a wide range of shapes and flavours, but it must always contain at least 10 per cent liver, with the best varieties containing over 25 per cent liver. *Braunschweiger* is a spreadable smoked liver sausage enriched with eggs and milk.

Rohwurst may be sold as sliceable sausages (salami, cervelat and garlic sausage) and spreadable sausages, such as *Teewurst* (very fine sausage) and *Pfeffersäckchen* (literally little pepper sacks). The best-known variety is a spread called *Streichmettwurst nach Braunschweiger Art*, which is made according to a traditional Brunswick recipe. Sausage spreads have more fat than their firmer counterparts for slicing, which makes them spreadable. *Katenrauchwurst* (smoked cottage sausage) is a coarse-textured, very firm sausage made almost exclusively from pork. It is smoked for a very long time, which results in a strong flavour; *Mettwurst*, made from mildly smoked pork and beef, may be fine or coarse in texture and some are soft enough to be spreadable. *Bratwurst* (grilling sausage) is also included in this category, although it is not cured. *Nürnberger Würstchen* is Germany's most famous mini grilling sausage.

Offal is also used in German sausages: *Sulzwurst* (brawn sausage) contains pieces of pork from the head or the leg, bound in a savoury wine vinegar jelly; *Zungenwurst* (tongue sausage) contains pieces of tongue and liver and is spiced with black pepper and sometimes paprika or nutmeg; it has a smoother texture than *Sulzwurst*. *Hertzwurst* contains pig's heart; *Truffel Leberwurst* is made with pork, pig's liver and truffles. *Mecklenburgerleberwurst* is made by mixing minced fresh pig's liver with lean, cooked, chopped pork and finely chopped kidneys, tongue and a little back fat. After being packed into casings, the sausages are boiled for 30 minutes, then left to dry, or are smoked.

Eastern Europe

In Eastern Europe, sausages in myriad forms, flavours and shapes are fundamental to the national cuisine. Some of the best known include:

Cevapcici have no casings and are made from a mixture of meats such as pork, lamb and beef. They are usually grilled or fried, and are popular throughout Croatia, Serbia and Bosnia.

Debreceni Kolbaszor Debrecener, named after the city of Debrecen in Hungary, is a heavily spiced pork sausage, usually unsmoked or lightly smoked, with a reddish-orange colour that comes from its paprika content.

Kranjska Kobasica is a Slovenian sausage made of pork shoulder, slab bacon, garlic and black pepper.

Kielbasa, the national sausage of Poland, is made in numerous varieties, from tender pork (a little beef or veal is sometimes added), fresh herbs and spices and then gently smoked for just the right amount of time to achieve the correct colour, flavour and aroma. *Kielbasa* is boiled, baked or grilled and eaten with fried onions, red horseradish (which is blended with beetroot) and mustard. It is also added to the filling for *pierogi*, crescent-shaped dumplings filled with potato, cheese or mushrooms. *Kielbasa* is also baked with sauerkraut and included in soups and stews – notably *Bigos*, the Polish national dish (see page 201). Also popular is *Kabanos*, a crinkled, slender sausage containing pepper and caraway, and *Szynka Sznurowana*, a hard, smoked ham sausage and a favourite throughout Poland (*szynka* is Polish for ham).

Lukanka, a smoked, dry-cured Bulgarian salami, traditionally made from pork, beef, veal, black pepper, cumin, salt, and fenugreek or caraway seeds, then dried for up to 90 days and smoked for up to four days.

Italy

The medieval sausage-seller was a familiar sight in Italian towns; a document from the Spanish Vice-regent in Palermo dated 30 January, 1415 shows that lamb, pork or sausages were bought 13 days out of the month while macaroni was purchased only once a month.

Fresh sausages are known as *salsicce*, but by far the largest and most important category of Italian sausages is *salami* and there are numerous varieties made all over Italy, with every province having its own traditional recipes and methods. The word comes from the Latin *salare* ('to salt') and every town has at least one salami specialist. Salami differs according to the type of meat used, the proportion of lean to fat, the way the meat is chopped, the flavourings and seasonings, the shape of the finished salami, and the length of maturing it receives. Generally, salami from southern Italy and Sardinia are spicier than those of the north. As a general rule, the thinner the salami, the thicker it should be sliced. Salami is the plural of the Italian *salame*.

Among the countless varieties of Italian sausages, the best known are:

Bondiola or *bondeina*, a large, round sausage from the Polesine area of the southern Veneto region, made with coarsely minced pork, beef, red wine, salt and black pepper. Sometimes it is smoked for a month or air-dried for two months.

Cacciatore is a small sausage made from coarsely minced, pure pork and cured for a minimum of three months. The name means 'hunter', as they were a traditional breakfast for hunters and easy to carry in their coat pocket.

Ciauscoli, a soft, dry, smoked sausage from the Marche region of Italy, is made from very finely chopped lean and fatty pancetta and pork seasoned with salt, pepper, garlic and wine. It is packed into a natural casing and then smoked for a few days over juniper berries, before being left to age for up to three months.

Coppa, made from the neck or shoulder of pork seasoned with herbs, spices, garlic and wine, is air-dried for at least six months. It has a delicate flavour and is always eaten raw and thinly sliced. Two particular varieties, *Coppa Piacentina* and *Capocollo di Calabria*, have Protected Designation of Origin (PDO) status (see page 115).*Coppa Senese*, from Siena, is made from pork seasoned with garlic, orange and lemon rind, cinnamon, caraway seeds and other spices.

Cotechino is an ancient type of sausage from Lombardy and Emilia Romagna. It is made from coarsely chopped pork rind (*coteca*), lean and fat pork, salt, pepper, cloves and cinnamon, then cured for a period of three weeks to three months. The tender, flavoursome sausage has a soft, almost creamy texture. There is also a version flavoured with vanilla instead of cinnamon. Fresh *cotechino* is usually boiled, although it is also sold precooked.

Finocchiona, fennel-flavoured Tuscan *salami*, gets its name from wild fennel (*finocchio*), the seeds of which are used to flavour this popular sausage. It is aged for up to 12 months and has a rich spicy flavour.

Luganega is a mild-tasting fresh sausage that originated in antiquity and was mentioned by the Roman statesman and philosopher Cicero (106–43BC) and the first-century Roman gourmet Apicius. The most famous *luganega* hails from the Lombardy region and is made from lean meat and fat, salt, pepper, cloves and cinnamon stuffed into a very long, thin casing. At one time, it was sold by length rather than weight. The sausage is sold coiled rather than twisted into links (like English Cumberland sausage) and in cooking is usually skinned, cut into small pieces and added to sauces and stuffings. It is also delicious split and grilled. In Basilicata, in southern Italy, it is called *lucanica* or *lucania*, and is flavoured with red chilli; it is usually served grilled.

Mazzafegati is a pork liver sausage containing pine nuts and flavoured with fennel and garlic. It originated in Norcia in Umbria, renowned for the excellence of its pork products.

Mortadella is perhaps the most well-known Italian sausage. The name may be derived from *mortaio* because the warm pork was originally pounded in a mortar to break it down; or possibly from the Latin *murtatu*, a sausage seasoned with myrtle. It seems to have originated in the city of Bologna and was mentioned in a document of the official body of meat preservers in Bologna in 1376 – the same year the Guild of Sausagemakers was formed. The largest of the Italian sausages, it can weigh up to 15 kg (33 lb) and is usually made from 60 per cent finely minced pork meat and 40 per cent fat in long strips, although *mortadella* may sometimes also contain beef or veal as well as pork. It is flavoured with spices and other ingredients such as pistachios, wine, sugar and olives, then packed into a synthetic casing and steamed until cooked. The best *mortadella* is *puro suino* (pure pork) and has the letter 'S' stamped on the casing. SB means *suino/bonino*, to indicate that it contains beef or lamb as well as pork. It is best sliced very thinly to bring out the flavour. *Mortadella di Amatrice* is a lightly smoked *mortadella* flavoured with cinnamon and cloves and aged for two months. It is made in Amatrice, a small town high in the Apennines between Lazio and Abruzzi.

Musetto, a sausage made from the meat of the pig's snout (*muso*), is a speciality of the Veneto and Friuli regions of northern Italy. The meat and some fat are finely minced and mixed with black pepper, cloves, nutmeg, cinnamon and sometimes coriander seeds.

Salama da Sugo, an ancient speciality of the city of Ferrara in northern Italy, is still an artisan product, as it is impossible to make on a large scale. It is made from pork tongue and liver, seasoned with salt, pepper, cloves and cinnamon. Some producers add a dash of red wine or Marsala. The mixture is wrapped in lean minced pork and stuffed into a pig's bladder, then bound and hung to dry for at least six months. It is cooked by simmering for about five hours, and is then cut open to serve. It is traditionally eaten with mashed potatoes.

Salame di Fabriano comes from the Marche region of Italy and is flavoured with a little garlic and black peppercorns, then formed in natural casings into shapes weighing up to 1 kg (2¼ lb). There's a strong tradition of pig-keeping in the Marches, and salami and cured hams are still produced in many homes. *Salame di Fabriano* was originally a pure pork salami, but is nowadays made commercially from a mixture of pork and *vittellone* – young beef (one to three years old), which has a superb flavour and virtually no fat.

Salame di Felino, one of the finest Italian salami, comes from a small town near Parma. It is made with the trimmings from the leg of pork used for Parma ham and with pork shoulder, seasoned with salt, whole black peppercorns, saltpetre, garlic and sometimes wine, and then cured for a minimum of three months.

Salame di Milano, made from finely minced pork seasoned with salt, black pepper and sometimes garlic, is soaked in red wine and enclosed in a casing about 8cm (3 inch) in diameter and then aged for at least three months.

Salame di Napoli is a pork-and-beef salami made from coarsely minced meat seasoned with salt, garlic and red chilli pepper, which distinguishes it from the milder salami of the north. The curing process lasts about four months and sometimes includes smoking.

Salame di Sant'Angelo, from Messina in Sicily, has its origins in the Norman conquest of the region in the eleventh century. Production ceased under Arab rule but resumed in the sixteenth century and has remained almost unchanged ever since. This sausage is unusual because it is made from various cuts of pork, which are sliced by hand into cubes and seasoned with sea salt and pepper; the sausage is then air-dried in the mountain air.

Salame di Varzi, a speciality of the town of Varzi near Pavia in Lombardy, is made from lean pork shoulder and pork fat, flavoured with red wine, salt, saltpetre and black pepper, and then aged for up to four months.

Salamella is also called Neapolitan sausage. It contains pork, veal, lard, red chilli pepper flakes, garlic, spices and wine and is lightly smoked. *Soppressata* is a pressed salami made throughout Italy. After being packed into its casing, it is placed under a wooden board, weighted down and pressed to eliminate air pockets (hence the name, which means pressed) and to achieve the traditional flat shape. It is then lightly smoked and cured for 3–4 months. *Soppressata* from Calabria is the most sought-after: it is made with 75 per cent coarsely chopped pork meat and 25 per cent pork fat, combined with garlic, paprika, pepper, blood, wine, salt and chilli. *Soppressa Veneta* is a large, soft *salami* from Valpolicella near Verona, made with 35 per cent fat.

Spain

The Iberian Peninsula and the Balearic Islands have similar sausages and an impressive range of *chorizos*, the best known and most popular of all the Spanish sausages. Seasonings and flavourings vary according to region and the individual producer.

Chorizo is, without doubt, the star of Spanish sausages and seems to have its origins in the Catalan region. It was originally a pale sausage and *chorizo blanco* (white *chorizo*), without paprika, is still made in some parts of Spain. The bright-red version dates from after the discovery of America and the introduction of the pepper plant into Spain, as one of its chief ingredients is *pimentón* (paprika), which besides adding colour and flavour, helps to preserve the sausage without refrigeration. There are endless varieties of *chorizo* – thick, thin, smoked or unsmoked, lean or fatty, all made from chopped or minced pork, pork fat, garlic and black pepper and salt, plus herbs, maybe a splash of white wine and the obligatory paprika or red peppers. A cured, air-dried sausage, it varies in spiciness according to the maker and is sliced and eaten cold or used as an ingredient for soups and stews. The finest are made from the meat of the Iberian pig. *Chorizo* are also made from the meat of wild boar (*jabalí*).

Butifarra describes a large range of sausages. *Butifarra blanca* is a cooked white sausage made from minced pork and spices. *Butifarra dulce*, a speciality of the Empordà region of Catalonia, is unusual because it is a sweet sausage, cured with sugar and flavoured with cinnamon and lemon juice and usually served as a dessert.

Jabuguito is a small *chorizo* that is eaten raw or deep-fried.

Llonganissa, Longaniza or *Llangonissa* is a long, thin pork sausage seasoned with paprika, cinnamon, aniseed, garlic and vinegar.

Lomo embuchado is a delicately flavoured sausage made from lean pork loin marinated in garlic, paprika, salt, oregano, nutmeg and other spices, then stuffed into a natural casing, tied and air-dried for at least six months.

Lomo Ibérico de Bellota is the dry-cured loin of the acorn-fed, free-range, Iberian black pig, packed into a natural casing, cured in salt, garlic, spices, and then air-dried. It is highly regarded and served in wafer-thin slices.

Morcón is a spicy sausage, made from chopped shoulder and loin meat from Iberian pigs, seasoned with salt, paprika, pepper and other spices such as cloves, then stuffed into a pig's intestine. It is air-dried for at least six months and is similar to chorizo.

Salchicha is the Spanish term for a fresh pork sausage popular throughout Spain and Portugal and is also called Longaniza if long and thin.

Salchichón is a cured sausage made from the lean, tender meat of Spanish white pigs that have foraged in the oak forests. The meat and fat are coarsely ground with spices, packed into sausage casings and allowed to dry. Traditionally, the sausage is cured outdoors on large drying racks for about 45 days, although many modern producers cure in a drying shed. *Salchichón* is spicy and speckled with fat, which gives it a slightly creamy texture. A particular type of *salchichón* from Catalonia is the prized *Fuet* ('whip' in Catalan), which is no more than 4 cm (1½ inch) thick.

Sobrasada is the most famous sausage of the Balearic Islands. A hot, spicy, soft, almost pâté-like pork sausage flavoured with garlic and paprika, it is made from the meat of the native black pigs, whose diet includes beans, carob, grasses, acorns and figs. The latter impart a perceptible, almost sweet flavour to the meat. The chopped or minced pork is mixed with hot paprika, salt and pepper, then stuffed into skins, tied with string and dried for several weeks. In the old days, the sausages were dried for 12 weeks, but nowadays this is done in special drying rooms and usually takes about seven weeks. Less expensive *sobrasada* are also now made from the meat of white pigs or a mixture of the two breeds. Authentic *sobrasada* will bear the label '*Sobrasada de Mallorca de Cerdo Negro*'.

Portugal

Chourico is the Portuguese spelling of chorizo. Made from brine-cured pork, garlic, pepper, red wine and paprika, it is usually smoked.

Linguiça is the national sausage of Portugal. The key ingredient of this mild pork sausage is vinegar, which gives *linguiça* a unique flavour. Other ingredients include wine or sherry, garlic, oregano, paprika and cumin.

blood puddings

Blood pudding, or black pudding, a mixture of pigs' blood and pork fat mixed with spices, herbs and seasonings, is in all probability the most ancient type of sausage and has long been regarded as a gastronomic delicacy. Blood puddings are believed to have originated in ancient Greece – a stomach filled with blood and fat, roasted over a fire, was mentioned in Homer's *Odyssey* which dates from the eighth century. The ancient Romans, fond of spicy foods, introduced their highly spiced blood puddings and sausages to the countries they invaded, and these foods quickly became popular.

Blood puddings were made in late autumn and through the winter, straight after the pig slaughter, to prevent the blood from coagulating and also because the blood was highly perishable.

EUROPEAN BLOOD PUDDINGS

Today there are numerous varieties of blood pudding made throughout Europe, which vary widely from region to region and also according to the makers, who jealously guard their recipes.

Britain

Long ago, spicy black puddings, studded with cubes of white fat, were a delicacy to be enjoyed on high days and holidays. The name is long standing, as is evident from a reference in the play *Like to Like*, by the playwright and satirist Ulpian Fulwell in 1568: '…puffing as hot as a black pudding'. The English variety is heavier than most other European blood puddings, being made with cereal in the form of oatmeal and/or pearl barley mixed with blood, pork fat, onions, flour and herbs and robustly spiced. Once made with fresh pigs' blood, many of today's blood puddings use dried blood instead, as this is considered more hygienic. I met a long-established Lancashire black pudding-maker who remembered as a boy being given the job of stirring the fresh blood into the rest of the ingredients. He told me that it was necessary to stir vigorously and constantly to avoid the blood clotting – and remembered it as very laborious work.

The different blends of herbs and spices account for the distinguishing flavours of each region's black pudding and may include mint, marjoram, tansy, celery seeds, coriander, caraway, pennyroyal, rosemary, thyme and savory. The mixture is packed into casings and simmered in water until cooked. Black pudding comes in various shapes and sizes: long or short lengths, ring, and horseshoe shapes – the latter is the traditional shape of black puddings from Bury in Lancashire, which are particularly renowned for their flavour. Bury black puddings are sold hot, ready to eat, in the town's market, sometimes split open and spread with English mustard. Although black puddings are sold already cooked, they are always fried, grilled, baked or boiled at home. Black pudding is a feature of the traditional British breakfast, along with bacon, sausages and eggs.

Recent additions to the black pudding market include a hot chilli variety with a definite 'kick'. There's also a black pudding ice cream, made by a Lancashire company for the annual Black Pudding Festival in Bacup in Lancashire; this is an innovative combination of vanilla ice cream with a touch of English mustard studded with pieces of black pudding. Paul Heathcote, an enterprising English chef, has created black pudding chocolates. The flavour combination isn't as strange as it sounds; in fact, the deep and intense flavours of the chocolate complement the rich, spicy black pudding well. In Italy and Spain, chocolate has long been used as an ingredient of rich meat and game dishes.

Scottish black puddings differ from English black puddings in that they don't contain large cubes of fat and are spicier. Those made in the Western Isles are particularly renowned for their quality and flavour and are called

marag dubh in Scots Gaelic. The puddings are most often seasoned with black pepper, cayenne, mace, coriander and herbs, then lightly poached for 5–10 minutes.

France

Boudin noir (black pudding) is very popular throughout France; in fact, the French are so passionate about their *boudin noir* that the Foreign Legion has a regimental marching song, 'Le Boudin'. There is even a brotherhood – the Confrérie des Chevaliers du Goûte Boudin (Brotherhood of the Knights of the Black Pudding) – which is pledged to conserve the varieties and associated traditions of *boudin* and that also sponsors an annual international tasting.

Lighter than the English version, French-style black pudding is made from blood mixed with pork fat, onions and cream; this is then delicately spiced before being poured into thick skins and boiled. Some regional *boudins noirs* may contain breadcrumbs, herbs, chestnuts, garlic, chopped apples or calvados. In the spring, some variations have finely chopped beet or chard leaves added. In Brittany, calfs' blood is added to pigs' blood to make *boudin*.

Boudin can be boiled, grilled or fried and is delicious eaten hot or cold. It's particularly good accompanied by caramelised apples, apple purée, mashed potatoes and a selection of piquant mustards; its earthy flavour also goes well with seafood such as scallops. In France, *boudin* is served with fruits such as apples, pears, grapes and rhubarb and is eaten at the *Réveillon* (the meal after Christmas midnight mass) and frequently at Easter. In Alsace the traditional Christmas roast goose is accompanied by black pudding and apples. *Boudin noir* also makes a tasty addition to pâtés and terrines and is sometimes used as a stuffing for pigs' trotters.

Galabart is a blood sausage made in southwest France, particularly in the Monts de Lacaune area (at the intersection of the Aveyron, Lot and Tarn *départements*). Pigs' blood is mixed with pork rind and the chopped meat from the pig's head, tongue, lungs and heart; bread is often added too. It is not put into a casing but into a pot and may also be canned or dried. It is served in thick slices, usually with a dash of wine vinegar.

Boudin du Béarn is another speciality of southwest France; it contains pieces of pork meat and is usually eaten cold. Blood puddings with black, red or white skins, flavoured with herbs and spices, are local favourites in the Lozère *département*, where *boudin* is made with blood, onions and

herbs and sometimes a splash of pastis. Some producers add pork meat and/or spinach to their *boudin*, but this is frowned on by purists. In the Loire Valley, *gogue* or *cogne* is similar to *boudin*, but is very large and is made with a large quantity of green leafy vegetables and herbs and a little pork, bound together with pigs' blood.

Italy

Biroldo, from Tuscany, is a very dark brownish-red, soft-textured, blood sausage containing lighter-coloured chunks of meat and fat and is traditionally made from parts of the pig (heart, lungs and tongue) that wouldn't be used for other sausages. The offal is boiled for a few hours, then chopped, seasoned and spiced with cloves, star anise, cinnamon, nutmeg, fennel and garlic and the blood is added. It is then packed into the pig's bladder or stomach and simmered for about four hours, after which it is cooled with weights placed on top to press out the fat. It can be preserved in lard for five to six months, or eaten fresh within 8–10 days. The *biroldo* made in Garfagnana differs from that made elsewhere, for in Garfagnana the pig's head is also used. *Buristo*, also from Tuscany, is a blood sausage made with pigs' blood, pork meat and fat, lemon and the Tuscan *droghe*, an ancient blend of spices, which differs according to each pig butcher (*norcino*), but which usually includes nutmeg, cinnamon and cardamom. After boiling, it is served in slices.

Pigs' blood is the only animal blood used in Italian cuisine. *Mazapane* (not to be confused with marzipan!) is a mixture of pigs' blood, pepper, salt, nutmeg, salt, cubes of fat, breadcrumbs, garlic and red wine cooked in the oven or in a bain-marie until solid. It is usually sliced and fried and served with onions. *Roventini* are fritters made by whisking together pigs' blood, egg yolks and flour and frying the batter to make pancakes.

Sanguinaccio dolce is a creamy dessert (*sangue* is Italian for blood), traditionally eaten at Easter in Naples. It was originally made by mixing pigs' blood with milk, raisins, sugar and spices; later additions included chocolate, pine nuts and candied fruits, which made the dessert very rich and dark. Fresh pigs' blood is difficult to obtain today, so unless it is made at home, melted chocolate is used instead of pig's blood. Another old speciality from Tuscany was a sweet black pudding made with chocolate, honey, almonds and candied fruit. A similar recipe combined pigs' blood with apples, flour, eggs, sugar, figs and raisins, which was then baked in the oven and eaten like a cake, warm or cold. A modern recipe from the Abruzzo region mixes pigs' blood with chocolate, orange zest, nuts and rum, which is cooked slowly for three hours, then left to cool and thicken before eating. *Migliaccio*, a thin pancake made from fresh pigs' blood, cocoa, lemon rind or candied orange peel and eggs, is a speciality of Tuscany.

Spain and Portugal

Morcilla (Spanish for blood sausage) was always prepared at the autumn *matanza* (pig-killing feast). *Morcilla* is similar to English black pudding and there are two main types: *de arroz*, containing rice, and *de cebolla*, which contains onion. The onion version is thought to be the original *morcilla* and it is believed that rice was introduced into the ingredients later to reduce costs (rice swells, while onion reduces). In northern Spain blood sausage is boiled and then smoked (usually over oak) to increase its keeping qualities. *Morcilla de Burgos* contains pigs' blood and fat, rice, onions and salt. The most famous *morcilla* is from Asturia (made from the blood of the local black pigs) and is an essential ingredient of *fabada* (see page 216), a much-loved bean stew with various meats, where the rich *morcilla* adds texture and flavour. *Fryela* is a blood sausage from western Asturia containing white beans, sugar and rice.

Boutifar, from eastern parts of Spain, is a blood sausage made from pigs' blood and fat; some meat is occasionally added. In Andalusia *morcilla* is made with almonds, pimentoes and parsley. A Catalan *morcilla,* called *Bull*, is made with breadcrumbs and may be either *negre* (black) or *blanc* (white) and is usually eaten cold. There is also a sweet *morcilla* from Galicia in the northwest Spain, with raisins and cinnamon, which is fried and served as a dessert.

Portugal has many varieties of black pudding, called *morcela*, which are similar to the Spanish *morcilla*.

Germany

Blutwurst is made from pork rind, pork blood and a cereal such as barley and is often smoked. After the pig was killed, it was traditional to eat *Blutwurst* in a meal called *Schlachtplatte* (slaughterplate), which comprised the fresh meat and sausages, accompanied by sauerkraut. *Blutwurst* are usually seasoned with a mixture of cloves, marjoram, thyme and cinnamon, which gives them a spicy flavour. Some blood sausages, such as *Rotwurst, Grutzwurst* and *Speckblutwurst*, contain other meats, offal, bacon or lard in varying proportions, as well as rind and fresh blood. *Thuringian Rotwurst*, known as the 'queen of blood sausages', originated in the eastern part of Germany and is one of the most popular and most common types of blood sausage. Other varieties include *Beutelwurst* (literally: sausage in a bag) from northern Germany, and the *Hausmacher Blutwurst* (made according to a traditional family recipe) that is also sold as an air-dried variety. *Zungenwurst* is a variant of *Blutwurst* that contains pieces of pickled pork tongue, but no cereal, and is spiced with ground black pepper. It is cured and dried, so needs no cooking and is often sold already sliced. Fried *Blutwurst* is traditionally enjoyed with a dish of sour-spicy lentils. A favourite German winter meal, *Himmel und Erde* (heaven and earth) – stewed apples and mashed potatoes – is usually eaten with *Blutwurst*.

Other European varieties of blood pudding

Throughout Eastern Europe, blood sausage is known as *kishka* (gut or intestine) and is made with pigs' blood and buckwheat. In Poland it is also called *kaszanka*; Poland also has a type of brawn made with blood known as *salceson* and *Brunszwicki*.

In Hungary, *Véres Hurka* is made with rice, pigs' blood and pork.

In Bulgaria, *Karvavitsa* is a combination of pigs' blood, fat, spices and mountain herbs. A similar blood sausage is also eaten in Serbia, Slovenia and Croatia.

Rumanians enjoy traditional *Sângerete* (from *sânge*, 'blood' in Rumanian), made with pork meat, blood, a filler such as cooked rice, and seasonings of pepper, garlic and basil.

Other varieties of blood puddings include *Blodpøls* from Norway and Denmark, and *Tongeworst* (with added pigs' tongues) from the Netherlands. *Blodpudding* is well liked in Sweden and is often accompanied with lingonberry jam. An historic dish seldom seen nowadays is *Svartsoppa* (black soup), a soup made from pigs' blood.

In Finland, *Mustamakkara* (black sausage) is a mixture of pork, pigs' blood, crushed rye and flour; finely chopped onions are added to the same mixture to form a batter that is made into pancakes, called *Veriohukainen* or *Veriletut* (blood pancake).

In Estonia, *Verivorst* (blood sausage) in a variety of shapes and sizes is a traditional Christmas food, often eaten with lingonberry jam and/or sour cream or butter.

BLACK PUDDING FESTIVALS

In many countries, devoted black pudding fans visit festivals dedicated to the time-honoured delicacy. In Ramsbottom, in the north of England, hundreds compete every year in the World Black Pudding Throwing Championships. The puddings are encased in ladies' tights and contestants hurl them at a 6 m (20 ft)-high stack of Yorkshire puddings. Whoever knocks the most Yorkshire puddings off the stack is declared the winner. The competition is reputed to date back to an incident in battle between the armies of the Houses of Lancaster and York during the Wars of the Roses.

In France, home of the boudin noir, traders and butchers have gathered every year in March for more than half a century in the picturesque village of Mortagne-au-Perche, in Normandy, to celebrate black pudding at the annual Foire au Boudin, or Black Pudding Fair. Black pudding producers travel from all over Europe to compete for the coveted award of 'International Best Black Pudding' and there are also demonstrations of boudin-making from local butchers and charcutiers. Visitors can sample the many tasty puddings, and there is even an award for the 'Best Black Pudding Eater' and a prize for the best pig squeal. So many puddings are consumed at the black pudding fair that, if laid end-to-end, they would stretch for 5 km/3 miles.

Pig-killing fiestas in November in the Andalusia region of southern Spain celebrate the annual ritual, giving thanks for the winter stockpile of *morcillas*, hams and sausages. In Mallorca, in years gone by, every village celebrated the *matança*, the winter slaughter of pigs, as a joyous occasion with singing, dancing and eating.

THE RECIPES

MAKING SAUSAGES

Well, I had to tackle it! There is, of course, a whole world of sausages and one could probably write an entire book on the subject, so all I intend to offer is a basic recipe and a method, a couple of variations, then a few ideas of other ways to use your wonderful, additive-free sausagemeat. Remember, a good sausage needs to be cooked slowly and good mash needs floury potatoes.

It is worth investing in the mincer and sausage funnel, as sausages are very easy to make, and by making your own you reduce the amount of unnecessary additives, such as rusk, preservatives, excess salt, and – my main horror – dried herbs! It is also possible to make sausages from other meats such as lamb and rabbit: replace the lean pork with other lean meat, but use the same amount of pork belly. Go on – experiment! And at least you know what's in them.

First, to make your sausages...

homemade sausages

MAKES 20–24 SAUSAGES

fresh sausage casings
1 kg/2¼ lb lean pork
1 kg/2¼ lb rindless,
 fat pork belly
fresh herbs such as sage,
 thyme and marjoram
1 tsp salt and pepper
lard or vegetable oil,
 for frying

You will need a mincer and a funnel; some mincers have a sausage funnel attachment.

Soak the sausage casings in cold water for 1 hour; this softens them and removes the salty preservative.

Mince the pork and pork belly with the herbs, salt and pepper to taste, then remove the mincer attachment and replace with the sausage funnel. Cut off a manageable length of casing, about 3 metres/10 feet, open one end, place it over the funnel nozzle and push it all onto the nozzle, then tie the other end off loosely so that air can escape. With the mincer set to low, gently ease the pork mix into the casing, making sure it's an even fill with no gaps. When the casing is nearly filled, remove from the nozzle and tie up the end, then tighten the other end to secure and twist into sausage lengths, about 10cm/4 inches. Repeat with the remaining casings and pork. Let the sausages dry on absorbent kitchen paper for about 10 minutes.

Pick out enough to feed 4–5 or however many you're cooking for. You can store the rest in the fridge for a few days or freeze them.

To cook the sausages, heat a frying pan with some lard or vegetable oil, then put the sausages in and cook on a medium high heat to brown them all over. Half-cover the pan, reduce the heat and cook for another 20 minutes or so – they will become lovely and sticky and unctuous. You can also cook them in the oven, at 200°C/400°F/gas 6.

homemade mash

FOR THE MASH
SERVES 4–5

1.5 kg/3 lb 5 oz old floury
  potatoes such as Maris
  Piper, peeled
100 g/3½ oz butter
150 ml/5 fl oz milk
  or cream and milk
grated nutmeg
salt and pepper

Cut the potatoes into even-size pieces. Place in a large pan and cover with cold water to about 2 cm/¾ inch above the highest potato. Cover with a lid and bring to the boil, then reduce the heat to a simmer and cook for about 20 minutes until a knife inserted into a potato slides in and out easily. Drain in a colander and return to the heat to dry out for a few minutes, shaking them to really let the moisture out.

Melt the butter in another pan with the milk or cream and milk.

Add salt and pepper to the potatoes and mash them with a potato masher. Then add the hot milk and butter mixture and beat in, check for seasoning and add a few gratings of nutmeg.

Serve on hot plates with the sausages on top. Very good with English mustard and, dare I say, ketchup or Mostarda, the Italian fruit preserve.

other sausage mixes

Wiltshire mix

MAKES 12–14 SAUSAGES

900 g/2 lb lean pork
100 g/3^1/$_2$ oz fresh breadcrumbs
^{1}/$_4$ tsp grated nutmeg
1 tsp salt
^{1}/$_3$ tsp ground black pepper
^{1}/$_2$ tsp each finely chopped fresh marjoram, thyme and sage
300 g/11 oz suet

Italian mix

MAKES 12–14 SAUSAGES

1 kg/2^1/$_4$ lb pork, 70% meat and 30% fat, such as leg
 and belly
3 tsp cold water
2 tbsp fennel seeds
1 tsp salt
^{1}/$_2$ tsp freshly ground black pepper

spicy sage mix

MAKES 20–24 SAUSAGES

1 kg/2^1/$_4$ lb belly pork
500 g/1 lb shoulder pork
1 tbsp ground cloves
2 tbsp ground coriander
^{1}/$_2$ tsp nutmeg
1^1/$_2$ tbsp salt
1 tsp ground black pepper
1 tbsp fresh sage, chopped

SAUSAGE AUBERGINE & COURGETTE

SERVES 2

2 large pork sausages
1 small aubergine
1 courgette
3 tbsp olive oil
4 slices crusty white bread
salt and pepper

Cook the sausages. Meanwhile, slice the aubergine into 1 cm/½ thick slices and the courgette lenthwise into four. Brush with olive oil and grill the aubergines for 10 minutes and the courgettes for 8 minutes, turning once, then drain on kitchen paper.

Place two slices of bread on a board and layer with the aubergine slices, then the courgettes; season with salt and pepper. Slice the sausages lengthwise and place on top. Place the remaining slices of bread on top, push down firmly and slice diagonally.

SAUSAGE LETTUCE & RHUBARB

The rhubarb relish is good with other foods such as cold pork. The sausages can either be cooked specially or they can be left over cold from the fridge.

Cut the rhubarb into 2.5-cm/1-inch pieces, wash and shake dry; place in a pan with a well-fitting lid, sprinkle on the sugar and the wholegrain mustard. Cover with the lid and stew gently over a low heat for about 15 minutes or until the rhubarb is completely soft. Stir well.

Place 4 slices of bread on a board, spread on the rhubarb relish, place the sliced sausages on top and cover with the lettuce; season with salt and pepper. Cover with the remaining slices of bread, push down and firmly, slice diagonally.

SERVES 4

Allow 1 sausage per
sandwich

FOR THE RELISH
4 stalks rhubarb
50 g/2 oz brown sugar
2 tsp wholegrain mustard
8 slices of bread to your
choice
crispy lettuce such as
cos/romaine, washed
and dried
salt and pepper

SAUSAGE SANDWICH

Whether it's a cold sausage sliced lengthwise with wholegrain mustard and crunchy little gem lettuce, or a hot sausage accompanied by an oozing fried egg, the sausage sandwich is a wonderful snack for any time of the day, any day of the year. My first hot sausage sandwich was in London at one of those tiny coffee shops whose window is filled with all sorts of sandwich fillings and breads. I never understood how anyone could make a living in such a place, but they do. Sausages offer infinite variety, not least with the sort of sausage used, so here are a few ideas:

APPLE & BEETROOT

Apple and beetroot are delicious together as a sharp clean fresh flavour and combine well with a rich sausage. A really good brown absorbent loaf is best, as the beetroot and apple can be wet. Choose any sausage you like, whether it's an ordinary cooked one as above or any of the thinly sliced prosciutto types from Italy or Spain.

Grate a fresh dessert apple and mix with grated cooked beetroot, then spread over your bread. Add your choice of sausage and cover with the another slice of bread. A thin layer of hot mustard or mayonnaise adds to the richness.

SERVES 6–8

500 g/1 lb 2 oz sausage
  mixture made as on page
  174, with 2 peeled and
  crushed garlic cloves
  added
A little flour, for coating

FOR THE DOUGH
125 ml/4 fl oz milk
$^{1}/_{2}$ sachet (1$^{1}/_{4}$ tsp)
  dried yeast
$^{1}/_{2}$ tsp brown sugar
250 g/9 oz strong
  white flour
grated zest of $^{1}/_{2}$ unwaxed
  lemon
$^{1}/_{4}$ tsp salt
50 g/2 oz butter, melted
2 eggs, beaten

To make the dough, heat the milk to lukewarm, add the yeast and sugar and stir to dissolve completely. Cover and leave in a warm place for about 10 minutes.

Put the flour into a large bowl and mix through the lemon zest and salt; make a well in the middle. When the yeast/milk mixture has a frothy head, pour it into the flour. Add the melted butter and most of the beaten egg (reserve a little to glaze) and mix well, using a wooden spoon or sturdy spatula – put the bowl on a damp cloth to stop it moving about while you do this. Turn out the soft, sticky dough onto a floured work surface and 'knead' with one hand, pulling and lifting for 5–10 minutes until it is smooth and elastic. Place in a lightly floured bowl, sprinkle with flour, then cover and leave in a warm place to double in size, about 1 hour.

Meanwhile, shape the sausage mixture into a thick roll about 20 cm/8 inches long. Roll it up in a double thickness of clingfilm and poach in a pan of lightly simmering water for 20–30 minutes; do not let it boil. Drain well, remove the clingfilm and leave to cool. Pat the sausage dry with kitchen paper, then coat lightly in flour.

Knead the dough gently for a minute or two, then chill for 15–20 minutes until it is firm enough to shape. Turn the dough onto a floured surface and gently pat it out to a square about 20 x 20 cm/8 x 8 inches. Place the sausage along one edge of the dough, about 5cm/2 inches in, then fold the dough over and press the edges to seal all round. Place in a lightly oiled loaf tin (about 20 x 10 cm/8 x 4 inches), seam-side down, cover lightly and leave to rise for about 20 minutes. Meanwhile, preheat the oven to 190°C/375°F/gas 5.

Brush the loaf with the reserved egg and bake for 20 minutes until the dough sets and colours lightly. Reduce the oven temperature to 180°C/350°F/gas 4 and cook for another 20–30 minutes, until golden brown.

Cut into 2 cm/¾ inch slices, discarding the ends, which won't contain any sausage. Serve with a tomato sauce (see page 260).

sausage in brioche

I first came across this when I was working in the Alsace region of France, and it was an interesting, simple dish, almost rustic in its appearance. Traditional brioche dough is very rich, with lots of butter and eggs; this version is less rich and I add lemon zest as a nice counterpoint to the sausage. Which brings me to the sausage: the traditional French recipe uses cured, cooked, garlic sausage but I think it works well with the basic sausage mixture (see page 174) — add some garlic to the mix as you mince it.

scotch eggs

It is interesting trying to find out where dishes came from and why. It has been suggested that this recipe has nothing to do with Scotland and that Scotch eggs are based on recipes from India or the Lebanon, in which eggs are cooked in a spiced, ground meat mixture. As regards the breadcrumbs, these are well worth making yourself from bread that has been dried and roughly processed in a food processor.

MAKES 8

10 eggs
700 g/1½ lb sausagemeat (see page 174)
a pinch of ground mace
125 g/4 oz dried breadcrumbs
groundnut oil for deep-frying
salt and pepper

Boil 8 of the eggs for 10 minutes, then remove and cool in cold water. When cold shell them.

Beat 1 of the remaining eggs with 1 tbsp cold water. Season the sausagemeat with the mace, salt and pepper. Dip a hard-boiled egg into the beaten egg and cover it all over with sausagemeat, pressing it firmly on with your hands. Repeat with the rest of the cooked eggs. Beat the remaining raw egg in a bowl, then roll the sausagemeat-covered eggs in it and then in the breadcrumbs.

Deep-fry in hot oil until golden brown. Drain well. The eggs can be served hot or cold.

sausage rolls

It is so hard to find a decent sausage roll these days since, even if the pastry is good, the sausage inside often is not. However, it's straightforward enough to make your own sausagemeat. This recipe uses puff pastry, which I admit I rarely make because the bought stuff is so good, but you can use homemade shortcrust pastry as well. Serve these either warm or cold – they're very good on picnics.

MAKES 12

200 g/7 oz puff pastry
flour for dusting
225 g/8 oz sausagemeat
 (see page 174)
milk

Allow the puff pastry to come to room temperature, then roll out, or unfold, on a lightly floured surface into an oblong and cut lengthways into two strips about 12 cm/5 inches wide. Divide the sausagemeat into two, then roll each half into a long roll the length of the pastry. Place each roll down one side of the pastry and brush the uncovered edge with milk. Roll the pastry over to form a log-shaped roll and press the edges together firmly to seal. Leave to rest in a cool place for 20 minutes.

Preheat the oven to 180°C/350°F/gas 4. Brush the roll with milk, then cut into 5 cm/2 inch lengths and place on a baking sheet. Bake for 30 minutes. Delicious hot or cold.

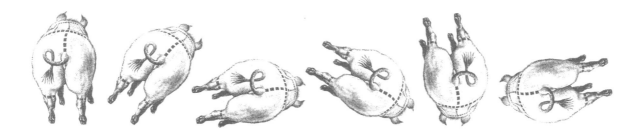

Spanish stew with tripe and chickpeas

An unusual combination of meats, and it's the kind of dish that might make a tripe-hater change their mind!

SERVES 4

200 g/7 oz dried chickpeas
350 g/12 oz fatty boneless pork (shoulder steak, for example), cut into small chunks
3 tbsp flour, seasoned with salt and pepper
2–4 tbsp olive oil
1 large onion, peeled and chopped
4–5 garlic cloves, peeled and chopped
225 ml/8 fl oz dry white wine
800 g/1 lb 12oz canned tomatoes
1 tsp hot paprika
900 g/2 lb tripe, cleaned and cut into 2 cm/³/₄ inch wide x 5 cm/2 inch long strips
225 g/8 oz whole chorizo sausages
salt and pepper

You need to start this the night before. Soak the chickpeas in water overnight.

Next day, toss the pork in the seasoned flour and shake off any excess flour. Put 2 tbsp of the olive oil in a large, heavy casserole pan over a medium heat, then lightly brown the meat. You will probably have to do this in batches to keep the heat in the pan. Remove the meat and set aside.

Add the onion and garlic to the pan, pour in the wine and stir to scrape up the bits from the bottom of the pan. Add the tomatoes and paprika and stir to break up the tomatoes. Drain the chickpeas and add to the casserole. Return the meat to the pan and add the tripe. Bring to the boil, then reduce the heat to a low simmer and cook on a very low heat for 1–1½ hours, adding a little water if necessary to ensure that the meats are always just submerged.

Add the chorizos, pushing them below the surface, and cook for another 30 minutes. Lift the chorizos out, cut them into thick slices at a slant and return to the stew. Check for seasoning and serve.

tortilla con chorizo

Eggs are perhaps as much of a staple part of the diet for many people as the household pig used to be, with the hens probably picking around the pigsty. It is therefore appropriate that many dishes combine eggs with pork products. We often associate the omelette with the Spanish tortilla, so it seems only right to include a version here.

SERVES 4

1 tbsp olive oil
100 g/3¹/2 oz chorizo
  sausage, cut into slices
6 eggs
50 g/2 oz cooked small
  white beans
black pepper

Heat the olive oil in a 25cm/10 inch diameter heavy-based pan. When hot, add the sausages and fry until hot through.

Beat the eggs and pour onto the sausages, then add the beans and pepper and, using a fork, quickly mix through. Allow to sit for a moment, then slide the tortilla out onto a pan lid, place a plate over the lid, invert and slide the tortilla back into the pan to colour the other side. Serve immediately.

olla podrida

This wonderful Spanish stew is not for the faint-hearted and is part of a long tradition of all-in-one-pot cooking, in which everything is cooked at different times in one pot. The French have pot-au-feu, which simply means a pot on the fire; in Scotland the traditions probably ran alongside the French and there is no knowing who did what first as the Auld Alliance stretches back many centuries. This Spanish dish has many variations, hardly surprising from a country that still has very distinct regional feeling. Some versions add cabbage, beet tops, green beans, hard-boiled eggs or spinach.

SERVES 4–6

300 g/11 oz dried
  chickpeas
250 g/9 oz stewing beef,
  cut into cubes
500 g/1 lb 2 oz pork
  spare ribs
1 pig's trotter
1 pig's ear
100 g/3½ oz piece
  of smoked bacon
100 g/3½ oz air-dried ham
1 onion, peeled and stuck
  with 4 cloves

1 bay leaf
2 carrots and 2 white
  turnips, peeled and
  cut into lengths
2 whole chorizo sausages,
  about 100 g/3½ oz each
2 blood sausages
  (*Morcilla*), about
  100 g/3½ oz each
2 garlic cloves, peeled
  and pulped)
2 tbsp chopped fresh
  flat leaf parsley
salt and pepper

You need to start this the night before. Soak the chickpeas overnight in cold water.

Next day, rinse them and place in a large casserole or pan along with the beef, ribs, trotter, ear, bacon and ham. Add water to cover, then add the onion and bay leaf. Bring to the boil, then simmer very gently, uncovered, for 2 hours.

Stir in the carrots and turnips along with the sausages and garlic and cook for another 30 minutes.

Lift the meats out and cut into small pieces, stripping the meat from the trotter and spare ribs, and discard the bones. Return all the meats to the 'olla' (pot), season to taste, add the parsley and serve.

meatballs in tomato sauce

Nick Piercy and his lovely Italian wife used to run a wonderful Italian restaurant in Falkland, Fife, called Luigino's. Nick showed me how to make these simple minced balls, which he served in the restaurant with home-made pasta and tomato sauce (see page 260). This recipe serves two, but you can increase the quantities if you would like to make more.

SERVES 2

125 g/4 oz minced pork
125 g/4 oz minced beef
3 tbsp fresh breadcrumbs
2 tsp grated Parmesan
1 tbsp chopped fresh flat
  leaf parsley
1/2 onion, peeled and finely
  chopped
1 egg, lightly beaten
salt and black pepper
1 tbsp olive oil
1/2 quantity tomato sauce
  to serve (see page 260)

Mix the minced meats with all the other ingredients except the olive oil, seasoning as you mix well. Roll into little balls – you should get about 8.

Heat the olive oil in a hot pan and brown the meatballs all over, then reduce the heat, add the tomato sauce and cook very gently for about 5 minutes, until cooked through. Serve with spaghetti.

pounti

This recipe originates in the Auvergne region of central France, but there's a good deal of variation within the region. Some cooks make it with a pancake batter, some add Swiss chard, prunes or raisins, and I have even seen it made with a partridge, which makes it similar to a chartreuse – a game bird cooked with cabbage leaves. But what most recipes have in common is the use of pork in various forms: fresh pork, ham or bacon. It's a sort of soufflé meat loaf.

SERVES 10

2 x 2 cm/³/₄ inch thick
  slices white country
  bread, cut into chunks
250 ml/9 fl oz milk
9 rashers of smoked
  streaky bacon, cut into
  small pieces
¹/₂ onion, peeled and
  roughly chopped
¹/₂ tsp salt
175 g/6 oz pancetta,
  cut into lardons
  (see page 87)
115 g/4 oz pork belly,
  minced
2 tbsp chopped fresh
  flat-leaf parsley
2 tbsp chopped chives
1 egg
140 g/4¹/₂ oz plain flour
40 pitted Agen prunes
black pepper

Preheat the oven to 200°C/400°F/gas 6. Grease a 20 cm/8 inch round baking pan. Combine the bread and milk in a bowl and set aside to soak for 10 minutes.

Meanwhile, cook the bacon in a pan over a medium heat, stirring frequently, until it has rendered its fat, about 8 minutes. Add the onion, salt, and pepper to taste and cook until softened, about 15 minutes.

Put the bread and milk mixture into a food processor, add the bacon and onion mixture, along with the pancetta, pork, parsley, chives and egg and whiz to a fine paste. Add the flour and pulse until combined. Scrape into a bowl and fold in the prunes. Transfer the mixture to the prepared pan, smooth the top and cover with foil. Bake in the oven for 30 minutes.

Remove the foil and continue to bake until lightly browned and a knife inserted into the centre comes out clean, about 45 minutes. Transfer the pan to a rack and leave to cool for 15 minutes. Cut into 2 cm/³/₄ inch thick slices and serve.

CHOUCROUTE

Traditionally in Europe, choucroute, or sauerkraut, was made with fresh cabbages cut after the first frosts of autumn. It was eaten with the fresh meat after the autumn pig killing, and it would then be used with a variety of dishes: salt pork and smoked sausage in the winter; fresh fish in early spring; or as a salad with chopped apples or raw onion.

Choucroute is made by layering finely shredded cabbage leaves with salt; juniper berries and/or caraway seeds are sometimes added for extra flavour. A weighted cover is placed on top to press the layers together. The cabbage ferments over 3–8 weeks, during which time the salt draws out the moisture and forms a brine. The cabbage develops a distinctive sour flavour and becomes light and crunchy and easily digested. It also has the benefit of being a rich source of vitamins and minerals. It is an excellent source of vitamin C and was often included in military rations, as it was generally believed that it prevented scurvy – a belief that was later proved correct when it was discovered that the acidity preserves much of the vitamin C present in the cabbage.

Choucroute garni is a traditional dish in the Alsace region of France and in brasseries throughout the country. In this hearty family dish, the choucroute is often cooked with a ham knuckle and pieces of smoked or salt pork, then served with the region's splendid sausages and boiled or baked potatoes. Various herbs or spices may be added (particularly juniper berries, which aid digestion), and sometimes goose fat, bacon fat, lard or oil are used. A regional speciality is choucroute royale, in which champagne or Alsatian crémant (sparkling wine) is poured through cooked choucroute.

homemade choucroute

Here is a recipe taken from Elisabeth Luard's wonderful *European Peasant Cookery*. If you want to make it yourself, try a smaller quantity of cabbage, say 5 kg/11 lb, and 50 g/ 2 oz sea salt. Instead of a wooden barrel, use a sterilised large glass jar or plastic bucket. For simplicity, omit the step about lining the barrel with perfect outer leaves: discard wilted leaves and the core, shred the rest and away you go! Use a ceramic plate with a weight on top to press the cabbage.

25 kg/55 lb cabbage
1 kg/2¼ lb sea salt

You will need a large wooden barrel with a lid and a weight. Make sure it is very clean and set it in a cool place on boards to ensure that air can circulate freely.

Trim off the outer leaves of the cabbages and save the perfect ones – you will need about 30. Line the bottom of the barrel with 10 of these. Slice each cabbage in two, then cut out and discard the solid stalk. Shred the cabbage hearts with a very sharp knife, as fine as you can. Mix the salt with the cabbage, then pack it into the barrel, pressing each layer down well. Salt the remaining 20 reserved outer leaves and place on top. Cover with a lid that fits inside the barrel, then weight it down well. Leave for 1 week.

After a week, check to see if a brine is forming – it should cover the cabbage. If not, make your own with 25 g/1 oz salt per 600 ml/1 pint of water and top up. Keep the lid and weight on to prevent the air getting to the cabbage. It should be ready in 2 weeks.

After removing sauerkraut from the barrel, make sure the remaining cabbage is covered by the brine, and wash the sides and rim of the barrel from time to time.

choucroute garni

This is a dish I used to see being cooked when I worked in the Alsace region of France. It was at the Hotel Anthon in Obersteinbach and the head chef, Michel Bering, had been sous-chef to one of my great culinary heroes, Roger Vergé of the Moulin de Mougins in the south of France. Michel was a great fitness fanatic and we would go cycling around the woods of the region on afternoons off from the restaurant.

SERVES 8

1.8 kg/4 lb home made sauerkraut or 2 jars of sauerkraut (about 900 g/2 lb each)
50 g/2 oz lard or bacon fat
16–24 mixed sausages, such as bockwurst, bratwurst, frankfurters and garlic sausage
8 pork chops – use smoked pork chops if you can get them
1 large onion, peeled and thinly sliced
1 green dessert apple, peeled, cored and sliced thinly
2 garlic cloves, peeled and crushed
2 bay leaves
10 juniper berries
1 tbsp caraway seeds
1 x 750 ml/25 fl oz bottle dry white Alsace wine
salt and pepper
lots of chopped fresh parsley to serve

Preheat the oven to 150°C/300°F/gas 2. Rinse the sauerkraut in cold water and squeeze dry. (The rinsing and drying reduces the weight by almost half.)

In a large casserole, heat the fat over a medium heat and brown the sausages and chops on all sides – do this in batches. Set them aside. Reduce the heat and add the onion and apple and cook until soft.

Put the sauerkraut into the casserole, then mix in the onion and apple. Add the garlic, bay leaves, juniper berries and caraway seeds and mix in well. Pour in the wine and about 225 ml/8 fl oz water to just cover everything, then bring to the boil. Add the pork chops, reduce the heat and simmer for 10 minutes. Cover with a lid and place in the oven for 1 hour.

Add the sausages and cook for another hour.

Check for seasoning, adding salt and pepper if necessary. Serve on a large heated oval dish with the cabbage in the middle and the meat around, and sprinkle with copious amounts of chopped parsley. Very good with steamed potatoes.

petit salé

A French stand-by, which will keep for weeks in the fridge. Effectively, this is home-cured bacon, and it's easy to prepare, but it's quite salty. You can use it in cassoulet, in soups and as a baster for lean game cuts – lay thin slices of petit salé on top of them during cooking. It's also delicious boiled and served with choucroute or lentils.

SERVES 8

2 kg/4¹/₂ lb piece of pork belly (it must not have been frozen)
¹/₂ tbsp peppercorns
¹/₂ tbsp juniper berries
1 bunch of thyme
3 bay leaves
500 g/1 lb 2 oz sea salt
15 g/¹/₂ oz saltpetre (if available)

Dry the meat well. Crush the peppercorns, juniper berries, thyme and bay leaves together, then mix with the salt and saltpetre, if you have it. Rub some of this mix all over the skin side of the meat, then the flesh side, then the skin side again. Sprinkle some of the salt mix onto a plastic tray or large plastic or glass container and place the meat on it, then sprinkle the remaining salt around it. Cover the meat with clingfilm, then place a clean plastic tray or board on top and weight it down with at least 1 kg/2¼ lb weight – I use bags of sugar, taking care that they don't come into contact with the salt mixture. Leave in a cool place, turning every few days.

It will be ready after 1 week: rinse off the excess salt, pat dry, wrap in clingfilm or greaseproof paper and store in the fridge, where it will keep for several weeks. To reduce the saltiness, soak the amount of bacon you need for your recipe in cold water for several hours before you need it.

Galician soup

This is a simple soup based on peasant staples – the end of a ham, and vegetable tops. If you don't have turnip tops, then add extra pepper and use the dark leaves of a spring cabbage or kale instead. It is interesting how sprout tops have become so popular with top chefs. I wonder if we will see a greater use of turnip tops coming in as well.

SERVES 6–8

250 g/9 oz dried small
  white beans
1 ham knuckle
2 litres/3½ pints water
sweet paprika
4 medium potatoes, peeled
  and diced
400 g/14 oz turnip tops,
  dark spring cabbage or
  kale, coarsely chopped
2 whole chorizo sausages,
  cut into small pieces
salt and black pepper

You will need to start this the night before. Soak the beans in cold water overnight.

Drain and rinse the beans and place in a large soup pot or casserole. Add the ham knuckle and water, then season with the paprika and salt and pepper to taste. Simmer for 1 hour.

Remove the ham bone, add the vegetables and sausages and simmer for 30 minutes. Serve hot.

bigos

Polish hunter's stew: If you want to be truly authentic, then you would have to look for Polish bacon and sausages, such as Wieska or Kilometrova. The idea of combining pork, bacon and sausage with mushrooms, honey and prunes makes it an interesting dish. I sometimes use chanterelles, dried by myself after forays in the Speyside hills, and whatever large spicy sausage I can find. It is always delicious!

SERVES 8

15 g/¹/₂ oz dried porcini
 mushrooms, soaked for
 15 minutes in warm water
1 kg/2¹/₄ lb jar of
 sauerkraut
250 g/9 oz bacon, cut
 into 5 mm/¹/₄ inch slices
2 onions, peeled and
 chopped
1 kg/2¹/₄ lb diced pork
 (shoulder is fine)
12 prunes
12 juniper berries
12 allspice
3 bay leaves
2 tbsp honey
3 tsp tomato paste
1 litre/1³/₄ pints pork
 stock (see page 259)
250 g/9 oz sausages,
 about 4 cm/1¹/₂ inches
 diameter, cut into
 bite-size pieces

You can cook this either in the oven or on the hob, but it does take a couple of hours either way, so you may prefer to use the oven. In that case, preheat it to 180°C/350°F/gas 4.

Take a large ovenproof pot, earthenware or similar, which can also come straight to the table. Place the sauerkraut in it and put over a low heat to warm.

Fry half the bacon in a frying pan to render the fat, then add the onions and cook until soft. Add this mixture to the pot with the sauerkraut and mix in.

Cook the rest of the bacon in the frying pan until the fat comes out and then brown the pork in it – this will need to be done in batches – adding a little lard or groundnut oil if the bacon doesn't produce enough fat. Add this to the pot, along with the prunes, porcini mushrooms, juniper berries, allspice, bay leaves, honey and tomato paste. Top up with the stock and bring to the boil. If cooking on the hob, reduce to a gentle simmer and stir from time to time, otherwise place in the oven without a lid for 1½ hours.

Add the chopped sausages, bring back to the boil and cook for a further 30 minutes until the pork is meltingly tender.

fricadeller

I worked in the Cotswolds for a while and we had a wonderful German chef who had married an English girl and settled nearby. Another chef in the kitchen came from Sweden and he introduced us to these delicious meatballs. Our German chef served them for lunch with tomato sauce, but this is not the Swedish way, where they are served with a creamy gravy.

SERVES 4

450 g/1 lb minced lean
  pork
3 slices of brown bread
1 onion, peeled and finely
  chopped
1/4 tsp allspice
1 egg
1 tbsp milk
2 tsp chopped fresh dill
salt and black pepper
vegetable oil for shallow-
  frying

FOR THE DILL SAUCE
4 tbsp soured cream
2 tsp chopped fresh dill

Mix together all the ingredients except the vegetable oil and form into 12 small patties. Leave to rest and chill.

Fry in the vegetable oil until golden on both sides and cooked through. Remove and keep warm while you make the sauce: pour off the fat and add a little water, the soured cream and the fresh dill. Stir to combine and heat through, then serve with the patties.

PÂTÉS & TERRINES

There are many schools of thought as to the difference between a pâté and a terrine, but it seems to me that a terrine is usually made in an oblong terrine mould and is often turned out and sliced, whereas a pâté is often served straight from the earthenware pot in which it has been cooked. Terrines are often lined in bacon and frequently have strips of other meats and nuts, and so on, running through them. You can create your own pâté once you have established a base mixture or farce. Of course, pork plays an important role in pâtés and terrines — many of them use both fresh and cured pork as well as the liver for flavour. Without the pig, we probably wouldn't have pâtés and terrines at all.

country pâté

This basic pâté is simple to make and can be varied by adding other ingredients, such as pistachios, chopped apricots, chunks of cooked ham or lightly sautéed chicken livers.

SERVES 8–10

2 tsp butter
1 onion, peeled and finely
  chopped
150 ml/5 fl oz brandy
350 g/12 oz lean pork
  from leg or loin
350 g/12 oz lean rosé veal
225 g/8 oz fresh pork fat
2 eggs, lightly beaten
1 tsp salt
¼ tsp allspice
¼ tsp chopped fresh thyme
1 garlic clove, peeled
  and crushed
2 bay leaves
4 rashers of streaky bacon
black pepper

Preheat the oven to 180°C/350°F/gas 4. Melt the butter in a pan, then gently sweat the onion until it becomes soft and translucent but not coloured. Add the brandy and simmer to reduce by half, then set aside to cool. Mince together the pork, veal and fat, then add the onion and all the other ingredients except the bay leaves and bacon. Mix thoroughly. To check for seasoning, fry a little of the mixture in a pan in a touch of vegetable oil until cooked, then taste and add salt and pepper accordingly.

Press the mixture into a 1 litre/1¾ pint terrine or earthenware dish. Place the bay leaves on top, then cover with the bacon. Cover with the lid, if you have one, or with aluminium foil. Place in a bain marie (see page 274) and cook in the oven for about 1½ hours. A long terrine will take less time than an oval-shaped one. To check that the pâté is cooked, push a skewer or thin knife into the middle of the pâté: the juices should run clear with little or no pinkness. Remove from the oven and the bain marie, place on a tray and remove the foil or lid.

Now, this next bit – pressing – is optional. If it's not done you will get a loose texture, but if you press the pâté you will get a good firm texture. Find a pan, dish or other item that is the size of the terrine (I often use a piece of wood wrapped in foil). Cover the top of the pâté with clingfilm, then place the pan or dish on top and add weights of up to 2 kg/4½ lb (you could use cans of food or bags of sugar, just make sure it is well balanced, otherwise you may have a sugar bag covered in pâté juices). Pressing pushes out some of the fat and firms up the texture. The juices will spill out onto the tray and can be discarded. Once the pâté is cold, you can refrigerate it without the weights.

The pâté is then best left for at least 24 hours before serving, but will keep for a week or more. To serve, either scoop it out of the dish, or turn it out and slice. Serve with toast or crusty bread.

pork and pistachio terrine

The addition of livers and cream gives this mixture a smoother texture. The pressing can be done in the same way. Between the two recipes, you can play around with your own ingredients to create your own pâté or terrine.

Serves 8–10

250 g/9 oz lean pork
125 g/4 oz pork fat
125 g/4 oz chicken livers
$^{1}/_{4}$ tsp allspice
a pinch of ground cloves
a pinch of ground nutmeg
2 garlic cloves, peeled and crushed
2 tbsp brandy
$^{1}/_{2}$ tsp salt and black pepper
1 onion, peeled and finely chopped
1 tbsp butter
2 eggs, lightly beaten
150 ml/5 fl oz double cream
50 g/2 oz shelled pistachios
200 g/7 oz streaky bacon rashers
225 g/8 oz thinly sliced ham
1 bay leaf

Preheat the oven to 180°C/350°F/gas 4. Mince all the pork and the chicken livers together with the spices, garlic, brandy, and salt and pepper. Turn out into a bowl. Gently sweat the onion in the butter until soft but not too coloured, then add to the meat. Mix in the eggs, cream and nuts.

Line a 1 litre/1¾ pint terrine with the bacon, keeping a little for the top, and press a third of the mixture into it. I find that, to get the mix into the corners, lifting one end of the terrine and thumping it down and then doing the same with the other end helps (it does make a bit of a noise, though). Put a slice of ham over the mixture, then repeat with another layer of ham, then a layer of meat mixture, then ham, then a final layer of the meat mixture. Lay the remaining bacon over the meat, stick a bay leaf on the top and cover with a lid or foil.

Place the terrine in a bain marie (see page 274) and cook in the oven for 1½ hours. The juices should run clear when a skewer is pushed into the middle of the terrine.

Ideally, the terrine should be pressed at this point. Remove the lid or foil (if foil is left in contact with the meat, it can taint the flavour, although it won't harm you), cover the terrine with clingfilm, and then weight it down as in the previous recipe. It is then best left for at least 3 days before eating. To serve, either scoop it out of the dish, or turn it out and slice.

Serves 12

3 young pigeons
groundnut or olive oil
200 g/7 oz fat bacon
350 g/12 oz game or
  chicken livers
2 tsp salt
a pinch of quatre épices
  (see page 274)
4 egg yolks
250 ml/9 fl oz double
  cream
2¹/₂ tbsp brandy
50 g/2 oz sultanas
black pepper

Preheat the oven to 240°C/475°F/gas 9.

Remove the legs from the pigeons – they can be used for making stock for soup. Season the birds and sprinkle with oil, then place in a roasting tin and roast in the oven for 10 minutes. Leave to rest for at least 1 hour, or overnight if you like.

Heat the oven to 200°C/400°F/gas 6. Put the fat bacon, livers, salt, quatre épices and a little pepper into a food processor and whiz to a smooth, creamy consistency. Add the egg yolks, cream and brandy and blend for about 30 seconds. Push the mix through a sieve to remove any fibres from the livers.

Rinse the sultanas in warm water and dry on absorbent kitchen paper – this removes any residue of sulphur preservative. Remove the breasts from the pigeons, skin them and cut into small dice. Mix them, along with the sultanas, into the liver mixture.

Pour the mixture into a 1 litre/1¾ pint terrine, cover and cook in a bain marie (see page 274) in the oven for 45 minutes to 1 hour, or until a thin skewer comes our clean and the juices run clear.

Leave to cool, then refrigerate – it will keep for up to 1 week. Serve straight from the dish with toast or crusty bread.

pig(eon) terrine

This is a delicious, smooth terrine, which, although it requires a bit of effort to make, has the texture of foie gras without the guilt! Serve with toast or brioche. When the recipe says fat bacon, it really means fat. I usually ask the butcher to cut a bit from the top of a whole side of bacon. If you can't get game livers such as pheasant or mallard, then use chicken livers instead.

rillettes

A traditional French potted meat, great for summer suppers with salads, pickled gherkins and olives. It's also good with toast or on a picnic with crusty bread. It keeps very happily in a cold larder for up to 4 weeks.

SERVES 4–6

1 kg/2 lb pork belly
4 garlic cloves, peeled
  and chopped
1 tsp sea salt
6 grinds of black pepper
  tsp each of ground
  nutmeg and mace
sprigs of fresh thyme and
  rosemary

Preheat the oven to 120°C/250°F/gas ½.

Remove the skin and bones from the pork and cut the meat into small cubes. Place in a large casserole with the other ingredients and cook for at least 4 hours; the fat should all have turned to liquid.

Drain off the fat through a sieve into a pan. Pound the meat in a pestle and mortar, shred it with two forks or process it in a food processor. Season well and then pack into small jars and allow to cool. Pour a little of the strained fat over the meat in each jar to seal. Cover and keep in a cool place – a larder rather than a fridge.

meat loaf

A British pâté, perhaps, made without liver. It can be served hot or cold, and if anything, is better eaten the day after you've made it.

Serves 6–8

350 g/12 oz back bacon
350 g/12 oz pork belly
175 g/6 oz fresh bread-
  crumbs
1 onion, peeled and
  chopped
1 egg, beaten
1 tsp mustard powder
1 tsp chopped fresh sage
8 tbsp dry cider
salt and pepper

Preheat the oven to 180°C/350°F/gas 4.

Mince the meats together, then add all the other ingredients and mix in well. Push into a 900 g/2 lb loaf tin, cover with foil and cook in the oven for 1½ hours.

Allow to cool a little before turning out. Very good served with tomato sauce (see page 260). If you want to reheat it, cover in foil and bake in the oven until cooked through.

G OTHERS

the often overlooked

The pig offers the greatest variety of offal, with every part of the animal being utilised in a range of tasty products. Together with its internal organs, the fat, head, ears, snout, trotters and tail were preserved in many different ways in the days before refrigeration. Every country developed its own unique ways of dealing with these parts of the pig, which gave rise to the wealth of delicious specialities.

Once regarded as inferior cuts, modern chefs are now eagerly embracing and including dishes such as brawn and faggots on fashionable menus. The variety of textures and flavours from these inexpensive parts of the pig make them a versatile choice for today's cook.

FAT

The pig has more fat than any other animals and through the ages this fat has proved enormously useful, both in the kitchen and as a medicinal remedy. The larger and fatter the pig, the more it was admired and valued, not solely for its meat, but also for its tasty fat. In parts of Europe, where fat was an important part of the diet, pig fat was often part of peasants' wages.

Health concerns about eating too much saturated fat are fairly recent and certainly would not have occurred to our ancestors, who would have considered it a crime to waste any part of a slaughtered pig and who held fat in high esteem. They spread pig fat on bread instead of expensive butter, and used it extensively in cookery. Fat is not only satisfying, it adds flavour, keeps food appetisingly succulent and juicy, and can also be used to fry food to golden crispness. Throughout Europe fat was, and indeed still is, indispensable for making sausages, which otherwise would be very dry and tasteless. It is also essential for basting dry meats and game to keep them succulent during cooking.

Pig fat is generally known as lard, from the Latin word for pig's fat *lardum*, and is white with a very mild, bland taste. Fat from different parts of the pig varies in quality and the speed at which it melts, so it was prepared separately according to type and used for different purposes.

Caul fat is the lacy white membrane surrounding the stomach and intestines. To use, soak the caul in warm water with a little vinegar, and then stretch it out gently (it tears easily). Pat dry and use to wrap game birds, such as pheasant or quail, calf's liver, or pâtés to baste them as they cook. English faggots (see page 241) are traditionally wrapped in caul fat and the French use caul (*crépine*) in a similar way to wrap *gayettes*, large meatballs made from pig's liver, pork meat and fat, which are a speciality of the Midi. They're delicious hot or cold.

Leaf or kidney fat (also known as flair, flare or flead) is the thick layer of fat around the kidneys and loin. It has a mild flavour and soft texture and is rendered separately from the coarser grades to produce fine lard, which makes particularly good pastry.

Back fat (from the pig's back) is hard and may be salted or cured like bacon for keeping, rendered for good-quality lard, or used for barding (see page 224).

Barding is a French term for wrapping thin sheets of fat around lean items to keep them from drying out during cooking. *Bardes* are thin sheets of fat used to line terrine and pâté moulds or to wrap lean cuts of meat. Threading whole roasts or lean items with thin strips of fat is referred to as larding.

Modern commercially produced lard can be made from any type of pig fat and is made by heating the chopped carcasses and meat trimmings with steam in a centrifuge, to separate the fat. The fat may then be further treated by the addition of bleaching and deodorising agents and emulsifiers.

Fat was generally rendered before it was used, to filter out any impurities, although leaf and back fat could also be used without rendering. To render, the fat was finely chopped and then heated gently, after which it was strained to leave the residue behind. It was poured into the cleaned pig's bladder and left in a cool place. The fat from around the internal organs and the belly was used to make a soft lard that had to be used quickly before it turned rancid.

Keeping the fat from becoming rancid was very important; after a few months, the stored fat in the jars would often have gathered bits of dust and soot from open fires, and it needed to be cleaned from time to time. The fat was put into a large bowl and boiling water poured over so that it melted. It was left to become cold and solidify so that any impurities could be scraped off the fat floating on top of the cooled water. In Asturias, in Spain, a ceramic pot of melted, rendered fat remains a culinary staple and is used to enrich stews such as *fabada* (which contains beans, *chorizo*, black pudding and pork fat) and other meat dishes and in baking both sweet and savoury dishes.

The residue – the crisp bits and pieces left in the pan after rendering the fat – were rolled in salt and eaten with bread in Britain, France, Italy and Spain. In England these pieces were sometimes put into a tart with brown sugar, spices, apples and raisins, then moistened with beer or wine and baked in the oven. Nowadays, these crunchy leftover scraps are sold in Britain as 'pork scratchings' (see page 258) and are a popular snack. Italians call these scraps *ciccioli* and in some parts of Italy they are included in bread dough to produce a very tasty loaf called *pane coi ciccioli*. In old Italian recipes, the crunchy morsels were finely chopped or minced and mixed into pastry dough. The French know these crisp, golden pieces as *grillons* or *grattons* and also eat them cold with bread or with a sprinkling of salt. In Spain, they are called *cortezas de cerdo*, or *cueritos* when they don't have any solid fat attached, and *chicharrones* or *torreznos* when they do. In Portugal, *courato* are popular snack foods sold from stands at large gatherings, such as football stadia. In the Netherlands, they were traditionally known as *kaantjes* but are now usually known as *knabbelspek*, which translates to 'nibbling bacon'. In Hungary they are known as *teperto* – or *töpörtyu* – and are a popular traditional food connected to peasant cookery. They are fried in lard and eaten piping hot with huge slices of bread and spring onions. In Serbia and Croatia, pork rinds are called *čvarci* and are usually deep-fried; they are a popular home-made peasant food. A special kind of *čvarci* unique to Serbia is called *duvan čvarci* (tobacco cracklings), which is made by pressing *čvarci* during the preparation, with the result that it looks just like tobacco.

Lard's mild, bland taste makes it ideal for use in baking cakes and breads – although tasteless, it produces a wonderful melting texture and bread was traditionally made with a small amount of lard to keep it moist. In England, splendidly rich and sticky Lardy Cake (see page 264) was popular in pig-rearing areas such as Wiltshire and Hampshire, where it was served on special occasions, particularly at harvest time in the autumn.

It was made by spreading a rectangle of bread dough with dried fruits (chopped apples were often added in orchard-growing regions), sugar, spices and lard and folding and rolling it several times before baking until crisp and golden. Lard also makes good crisp pastry and is essential for making hot water pastry, used for raised pork pies (see page 256). It was once very popular for frying, as it leaves no smell and has a very high smoke point of 205°C/400°F, but its use has been superseded by vegetable oils, with their healthier image.

In Spain, lard is used to make traditional biscuits such as *polvorones*, which gives them a delicate, tender, melting texture. Some modern recipes use butter instead of lard, which results in a completely different flavour and texture. *Mantecados*, rich, crumbly cakes synonymous with Christmas in Spain, are also made with lard. Their name translates as 'made from fat' because they are traditionally based on pork fat and *manteca* is the Spanish word for fat; '*manteca de cerdo*' and '*manteca de cerdo Ibérico*' means 'fat of pig' and 'fat of Iberian pig' respectively. *Ibérico* pigs are a special breed and when fed on a diet of acorns, yield a very flavoursome, less calorific fat, which, incidentally, makes wonderfully crisp roast potatoes.

Griebenschmalz or *Grammelfett* is a German and Austrian speciality that consists of the rendered fat and the crisp remains from rendering combined with apples, onions and spices, to make a tasty paste, which is spread on crisp sourdough or rye bread. *Grieben* are the tasty solids left after rendering the lard. *Rückenspeck* is a piece of back fat that is cured and smoked and is used in sausages or to wrap around lean meat and game or to spread on bread. Germans enjoy traditional fritters called *schmalzgebackenes*, which translates as 'something fried in lard'.

In medieval France, pork fat in all its forms was widely used in the kitchen for frying, to enrich soups and stews and to bard lean meat, and was even grated into fish pies to enrich them. A pork fat market used to be held on the day before Easter in front of Nôtre Dame cathedral in Paris. One popular delicacy sold from the stalls was peas dressed with pork fat. The celebrated seventeenth-century chef La Varenne is credited with publishing the first true French cookbook, which includes the earliest known reference to a *roux* made with pork fat. A piece of belly fat remains an essential ingredient of the cassoulets, daubes and garbures of southwest France, where it imparts its inimitable unctuous flavour.

In Italy, lard is called *strutto* if referring to the clarified pork fat that English speakers call lard, and *lardo* if it is cured pork fat. Pearly white *lardo* is an ancient delicacy, and every region in Italy has its own particular method of making this flavoursome speciality. After the pig is killed, the fresh fat is first soaked in brine, then usually rubbed with salt, herbs and spices (every producer jealously guards their secret blends) and hung for a few months before use. In the past, the valuable fat was kept for as long as possible and it gradually turned yellow. It was melted into soups and broths, included in pies and roasts, and used to dress vegetables.

Lardo crudo is a purée of pork fat creamed with herbs, seasonings and spices to a buttery consistency. In Piedmont, it was customary to preserve fresh salami in pure pork fat. *Salame d'la duja* ('*duja*' is the typical narrow-necked, terracotta container it used to be made in) is a spicy sausage cured for about eight months to develop its aromatic flavours. The warm liquid fat is poured over the pure pork sausages in pots, and the fat then sets, keeping the sausages preserved for up to a year.

Lardo di Arnad is from the small town of the same name in the Aosta Valley, in northwestern Italy, and is renowned for its superb flavour and melting texture. It is delicious sliced thinly and sprinkled with black pepper, or served with black bread and honey. It is made with fat from the backs and shoulders of local pigs, which have a very thick layer of fat; pigs that are at least nine months old, weighing a minimum of 160 kg (353 lb). The pigs must come from various regions in northern Italy: Valle d'Aosta, Veneto, Lombardy, Piedmont or Emilia-Romagna. After curing with salt, pepper and rosemary, the fat is left to dry and age in vats. Traditionally, the vats were made of chestnut or oak wood, but now they are plastic or stainless steel.

Lardo di Colonnata is the delicious aromatic *lardo* produced in the small village of Colonnata in Tuscany, using techniques that date back to antiquity. The fat is layered with diced garlic, rosemary, sage, oregano, salt and pepper in marble vats (*concas*) that have been rubbed with garlic, and is then matured for at least six months and up to 2 years. Originally this was done in caves cut out of the same marble stone but nowadays is also done in cellars. During this time, the salt draws the water out of the fat, leaving it white with a firm but creamy texture. The cheap, filling, high-calorie fat was ideal food for the hardworking stonecutters who hewed the stone in the quarries. Michelangelo (1475–1564) is reputed to have enjoyed this delicacy when he visited the marble mountains to select blocks for his sculptures.

Lardo production suffered a major decline in 1996, when EU health inspectors decided that the centuries-old methods of production were dangerous and implemented arduous regulations. In fact, the salt draws the water out of the fat, forming a brine, which makes it impossible for bacteria to grow. Fortunately, the Slow Food movement came to the rescue and protected and regulated *lardo* production by small artisan producers, making it one of the first traditional Italian foods to be protected under the *Arca del Gusto di Slow Food*. Today it is made in the time-honoured way and cured with local fragrant herbs and is much sought-after for its unique flavour and soft silky texture.

The product was granted European PGI status (see page 113) in 2004. The *lardo* must be produced entirely in Colonnata, the pigs must weigh at least 160 kg (353 lb) at the time of slaughter, the herbs and spices used must be fresh and the ageing period may not be less than six months. In addition, the *lardo* must be strictly connected to the region with the main ingredients being local in origin. The *lardo* regulatory board is closely linked to another that safeguards the *Cinta Senese*, the only race of Tuscan pigs to have survived extinction.

Lardo is best sliced very thinly and served at room temperature with crusty bread or toast. It has become a popular tourist attraction, with people visiting Colonnata just to taste it. Each year there's a festival to celebrate this traditional Tuscan speciality, the *Sagra del Lardo*, held on 25–26 August.

In Central and Eastern Europe, cured pork back fat is called *salo* and is similar to *lardo di Colonnata*. *Salo* is a very popular traditional food, as it is the perfect comfort food during the harsh cold winters. Peasants ate *salo* with bread to sustain them while working in the fields. *Salo* (as applied to this type of cured fat) is often mistranslated into English as 'bacon' or 'lard', but unlike bacon, *salo* has little or no meat; however, and rather confusingly, low-meat, high-fat bacon is also known as *salo*.

Salo is also known as *szalonna* in Hungary; *słonina* in Poland; and *slanina* in the Czech Republic. In Eastern Europe, *salo* may be salted or brine-fermented, while that of Central Europe is usually cured with a thick layer of paprika, black pepper or other seasonings. In some regions, *salo* maybe smoked. The slabs of fat are cut into manageable pieces and smeared with salt, then placed skin-side down into wooden boxes or barrels, layered with salt and aged in a dark, cold place, where they will last for a year or more.

Thinly sliced *salo* on rye bread rubbed with garlic is a traditional snack to accompany vodka in Russia, or *horilka* (Ukrainian vodka) in Ukraine. It can also be fried or finely chopped with garlic as a condiment for *borscht* (beetroot soup). Small pieces of *salo* are added to some types of sausage. *Salo* is often chopped into small pieces and fried to render the fat for use in cooking, and the remaining crunchy pieces (*shkvarky* in Ukrainian) are eaten with fried potatoes or dumplings (*varenyky*). The thick pork skin that remains after using the *salo* fat can also be added to the stock for soup or *borscht* and discarded before serving.

Salo is so popular in the Ukraine that it is practically a national dish, to such an extent that songs and poems have been written about it. *Salo* festivals are held in Ukraine every October and include *salo*-eating contests and huge *salo* sandwiches. The biggest *salo* sandwich, or *Salburger*, as it was called, was included in the *Ukrainian Records Book* and *The Guinness Book of World Records* – it was made from 105 kg (231 lb) of *salo* and 180 loaves of bread and measured 28.7 square metres (309 square feet) and took the world record for a sandwich.

In Eastern European jokes, *salo* is often represented as the highest object of desire for the stereotypical Ukrainian. A long-standing joke is the expression 'chocolate-coated salo' (*salo v shokoladi*), referring to an eclectic mix of tastes or desires. But the joke became a reality in the early 1990s, when a restaurant in Lviv made the dish as a novelty and a confectionery company later began producing *Salo v Shokoladi*. The finger-sized bars are wrapped in red foil and depict a Ukrainian Cossack with a moustache munching on a piece of *salo*.

Besides its value in the kitchen, pork fat was also employed as a medicine. In the sixteenth century, Sir Francis Bacon claims to have cured his warts by rubbing them with pork fat that afterwards was hung in the sun – as the fat melted, the warts disappeared. Lard mixed with herbs was rubbed into the chest and throat to cure coughs and colds in country medicines. Skin diseases were also treated with lard mixed with aromatic herbs. Pigs' lard was one of the remedies for 'Saint Anthony's Fire', a painful skin disease named after the saint. In Italy, shingles is still referred to as 'Saint Anthony's Fire'.

OFFAL

The word offal (from a Middle English word literally meaning 'off fall') encompasses all the internal organs: the liver, kidneys, heart, intestines, tongue, brain, tripe, as well as the trotters, ears and tail. Lean, nutritious and inexpensive offal offers a fascinating variety of unique and textures. In recent decades it has become very chic in fashionable restaurants.

The ancient Greeks and Romans relished offal and made the most of every part of the pig's organs. The teats, wombs and udders of sows were exclusive titbits reserved for Roman feasts. Romans were especially fond of the ears, cheek, jaw, snout and tongue and considered them delicacies. These gelatinous cuts were known as 'boiled meat' due to the fact that they were boiled for a long time and served in soups. When the soup was cold, it set to a stiff jelly and was often eaten sliced. Pigs' tongues were also boiled with wine, onion and herbs and served with a piquant sauce.

Another ancient Roman delicacy was *ficatum*, a type of foie gras made from the liver of a pig that had been force-fed with dried figs. The fattened liver was marinated in *garum* (a highly salted, fermented fish sauce) and spices, wrapped in caul and roasted. A later, rather curious recipe gave instructions for slowly cooking pig's liver, then mixing it with crumbled rich spice cake, toasted almonds, pine nuts, chopped belly pork, lemon zest, vinegar and sugar. This was left to cook and then mint was stirred in just before serving.

The development of commercial bacon-curing in Europe during the nineteenth century led to an increase in the availability of pig offal. Butchers in London at the time were very enterprising, claiming to use every part of the pig, 'except its squeak'. Pigs' ears were a popular snack; after singeing, they were simmered with salt, carrot and onion and sold cooked. Another popular dish sold by butchers was 'pig's fry', the heart, lungs, liver and any other offal – it was sliced, rolled in flour, seasoned and fried.

The sweetbreads (throat and pancreas) were once considered delicate foods suitable for invalids. They were soaked in brine, boiled in fresh water until tender and white, then drained and trimmed of skin and gristle and sliced thickly. Nowadays they are much sought-after by gourmets.

In England, faggots (the word means 'bundle') are an old, traditional way of using pig's offal. The liver, heart and spleen were finely ground, mixed with pork fat, herbs, spices and seasonings, formed into patties and wrapped in caul fat. Faggots are still enjoyed today (see page 241), baked or fried and eaten with mushy (puréed) peas as a cheap tasty meal. In the northern English counties of Lancashire and Yorkshire, faggots are also known as 'savoury ducks'.

Haslet is similar to faggots, although it is usually eaten cold. Cooked brined pork and offal is highly seasoned and shaped into a long loaf, sometimes wrapped in caul, then cooked and sliced. In the past, haslet was also put into pies.

Chitterlings are the small intestines of pigs. They are often used as sausage casings, and some butchers sell them cleaned, boiled and cut into short lengths or plaited, ready to be served in various ways. They can be eaten cold with mustard or vinegar, or fried with bacon or coated in batter and fried. Some butchers press them in a mould after boiling, when the liquid surrounding them sets to a jelly.

In the past, the bones weren't wasted – they were pickled in brine and used to flavour soups and stews. Salted pig's tail is used to flavour soups and stews in the Caribbean.

Brawn (known as head cheese in the United States) was made soon after the pig killing. The head, tail and trotters were cleaned, brined and highly seasoned, then boiled with onions, herbs, spices and vinegar until the meat could easily be picked off the bones. This was then either pounded to a paste in a large mortar or chopped finely, before being set into a jelly made from the cooking liquid. How long brawn would keep depended largely on the salt and vinegar content of the jelly, but even in cold weather it had to be eaten within weeks.

In medieval England, brawn made from a boar was regarded as a delicacy and was sometimes served with a sweet, spiced wine syrup. Some feast dishes were very elaborate: for *Mawmeny Royal*, shredded, cooked brawn was mixed with pine nuts, almond milk, currants, cooked, puréed quince, egg yolks and a great many spices. It was put into a dish and a wine sauce containing aqua vitae (eau de vie) was poured over it, before it was set alight and served flaming spectacularly. Later, it became usual to serve brawn acccompanied simply by mustard.

Off cuts:
1. Trotter
2. Liver
3. Heart (page 227)
4. Kidneys (page 228)

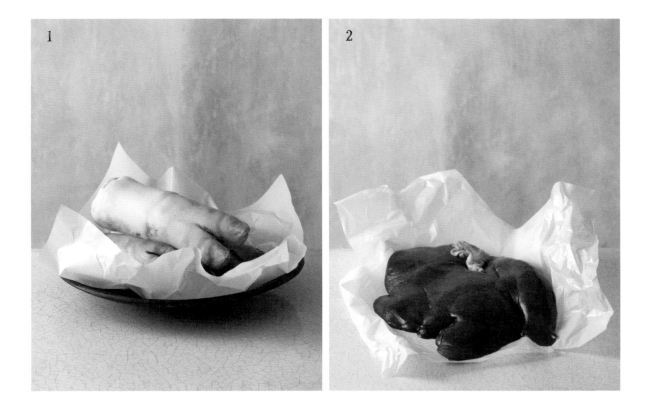

BARDING

Barding means wrapping fat round meat. The original reason for doing this was to protect the outside of large pieces of meat from drying out and over-cooking into a hard leathery texture during spit-rasting.

Some people feel that with today's lean meats it is necessary to add fat whilst cooking; indeed a neatly barded piece of meat does look impressive. Pork back fat is often used with other meats such as venison, which is inherently lean and prone to drying out. One might also consider caul a sort of barding when it is used for wrapping meat. Modern recipes for poultry or fish wrapped in prosciutto or bacon helps to add flavour as well as keeping the flesh moist. I often use streaky bacon when roasting a pheasant; it helps to protect the breasts whilst cooking in the early stages and then makes a delicious crisp 'extra' on the plate when serving. Try wrapping prosciutto round a chicken breast or salmon fillet and poaching in a little stock or wine. The chicken or fish is kept moist and the flavour is imparted to the meat.

Herb-roast pork

Here is an idea for a piece of boneless lean pork or veal,
which also tucks herbs under the fat.

Take a 900g/2 lb piece of lean pork or veal, dry it well and season with salt
and pepper. Brown lightly all over in a hot pan with a little vegetable oil.
Place 340g/12 oz of thinly sliced pancetta on a board overlapping the slices
and some sprigs of fresh marjoram or oregano, and wrap the meat in this,
tying it up with string. Roast in a hot oven 220°C/425°F/gas 7 for
40–50 minutes and then allow to rest for 15 minutes. The meat will have
retained more moisture than normal, and have a lovely extra flavour.
However, I still think that having a decent bit of fat on the pork
to start with is still better.

Trotters (pigs' feet) need long, slow cooking to make them tender and can be boiled or braised or boned and stuffed. As trotters cook, the connective tissue they contain softens and exudes a great deal of gelatine, so they make a good addition to stews, where the gelatine thickens the liquid. Gelatine also gives a good set to meat pies.

In Ireland, salted pigs' feet are called *cruibíns* (pronounced crubeens). In the past, these were sold in the streets, ready to be cooked at home. Cooked *cruibíns* could be bought in public houses (often together with soda bread and cabbage) since the salty meat encouraged thirst.

In France, offal is included in charcuterie such as terrines, brawn (fromage de tête, or 'head cheese'), galantines, pâtés, rillettes and confits. These products, originally intended as a way of preserving meats before the advent of refrigeration, are nowadays highly valued for their flavour and texture. Every region in France has its own wonderfully tasty and economical dishes based on offal.

Charcutiers (sellers of charcuterie) often boil the gelatinous trotters to prepare jellies for terrines. They may also sell pigs' trotters ready-crumbed (pieds panés) – they just need reheating at home. The crisp coating of soft succulent meat are a mouth-watering combination. A very old method of cooking trotters, unique to the Champagne region of France, is *Pieds de Porc Ste Menéhould* (see page 254–55). It is reputed that King Charles VII enjoyed this dish back in 1435. The pigs' feet are usually served with pickles, onions and mustard or with Ste Menéhould sauce, made from mustard, onion, vinegar and herbs. The classic recipe dictates that the pig's trotters should be braised for around 40 hours until meltingly tender, when the small bones will literally melt in the mouth. The cooked trotters are sometimes coated with breadcrumbs and fried in butter until golden.

Pouteille, a mixture of pork trotter meat, beef, wine, salt, pepper and spices, hails from La Canourgue, a small village in the northern Languedoc region, and is traditionally enjoyed on Sundays and holidays. In the past, families took the dish to the local baker to cook slowly in the bread oven, but nowadays it is sold in delicatessens. Another gastronomic speciality of the region is *fricandeaux* – small pâtés of pork and offal flavoured with salt, pepper, herbs and garlic. It's delicious eaten warm or cold as a starter.

An Italian speciality, *fegatelli* (liver wrapped in caul fat and then fried or grilled) is remarkably similar to faggots. Pig's liver and heart are both commonly used in southern Italian cuisine, in *ragus* as well as *fegatelli* . The spleen (*milza*) forms the basis of a speciality from Palermo in Sicily. It is grilled over charcoal, then very thinly sliced and fried in olive oil with chilli and served in a bread roll.

3

4

Zampone are pigs' trotters stuffed with a mixture of minced pork, pork rind, fat, salt and spices. It is believed to have originated in Modena in northern Italy, but has been enjoyed throughout the country since the nineteenth century. Traditionally, it is consumed mainly in the winter months, particularly at Christmas. It has a pleasant gelatinous consistency and every bit is eaten, including the casing. There are two kinds of *zampone*, precooked and raw; the latter are cooked at home and have the best flavour.

In Germany, offal is more popular in the southern part of the country than in the north. *Sulze*, a German speciality of cubed pork snouts in spiced gelatine with diced pickles and carrots, is usually served cold with a side dish of fried potatoes.

Serbians traditionally eat pig's cheek on special occasions, particularly at New Year. The tough meat needs long, slow cooking to tenderise the fibres into a gelatinous softness.

Olla podrida (see page 188) is a popular dish in Spain. It dates back to the Middle Ages, when it was called olla *poderida*, where '*poderida*' meant 'powerful' (*olla* refers to stew or to the stew pot), a reference to the powerful ingredients that it included, or possibly because it was a dish for only the rich and powerful. Eventually the 'e' disappeared and left the word '*podrida*', which unfortunately means 'rotten.' *Olla podrida* is particularly good when made with the fine red beans of Ibeas de Juarros, although chickpeas are used in many recipes. The beans are cooked in a clay pot for several hours (hence its name) until they become soft. The next step is to add the 'powerful' ingredients: bacon, *morcilla* from Burgos, *chorizo*, and the ribs, ears, and snout of smoked pig. The dish sometimes includes *la bola* or stuffing. It is eaten as a main course, although it is usual to serve beans first and then the meats separately.

Spain is another country that proves itself on using every part of the pig. The aftermath of the *matança* (pig killing) in Mallorca was *frit mallorqui*, a fry-up of the perishable offal with potatoes, onions and tomatoes. It can be found on restaurant menus along with *tumbet*, a baked dish of aubergines, potatoes, tomatoes, peppers and garlic. Butchers' shops throughout Spain display pigs' trotters (*manitas de cerdo, codillo de cerdo*) and they are featured on many restaurant menus – boiled, braised or stuffed with meat and roasted. A recipe from southern Spain is on page 253. In Catalonia, pigs' feet are also traditionally eaten with snails.

Pork pies

Quintessentially English, pork pies are admired all over the world. A crisp, golden-brown crust encasing a mouth-watering filling of chopped, seasoned pork in clear, glistening, savoury jelly, pork pie is one of the great triumphs of British cuisine and has remained virtually unchanged since its creation. Pork pies are always eaten at room temperature and are staples of hunt breakfasts and picnics.

The origins of the pie lie in the ancient Roman practice of wrapping meat or fish in a protective flour and water paste during cooking, which was discarded before eating. This coarse paste, known as 'huff' paste, was not intended to be eaten, but was meant to seal in the juices and flavour of the meat and, when cooked, act as a barrier against contamination. Huff pastry was removed just before serving and was given to servants and beggars, who considered the pastry, soaked in the tasty meat cooking juices, a rare treat in their frugal diet. Later, the pastry became richer and was intended to be eaten along with the filling. It's not known when fat (butter, lard or suet) was added to the paste, but the resulting crisp, tasty crust led to the development of pies, which were already a firm favourite in twelfth-century England and were also mentioned by Chaucer in *The Canterbury Tales*. The word 'coffin' or 'coffyn' referred to the pastry case, which was made in advance. A richer pastry was used to make small pasties served at feasts, such as Chastletes, small pastry castles filled with pork or almonds and coloured with saffron or sandalwood.

Early medieval recipes gave no instructions for making the pastry for pies and merely specified 'strong dough'. Fifteenth-century cookbooks gave the ingredients as coarse flour, suet and boiling water, which is very similar to the hot water crust used for raised pork pies today. Raised pies are so called because the warm pastry is shaped by hand and raised around a mould. The pastry can also be used to line specially shaped tin moulds. The firm dough can be moulded easily, and was often used to make elaborate decorations for raised pies.

A shortage of wheat in England in the late eighteenth and early nineteenth centuries, due to the Napoleonic Wars, resulted in flour becoming expensive and many cooks economised by making pies without a pastry crust. Ovenproof dishes imitated the decorative pastry crust and became known as 'piecrust' pottery. Nineteenth-century Wedgwood and Spode piecrust pottery, frequently decorated with reliefs of game and a rabbit finial, command high prices today.

Pie-making resumed when flour again became available and affordable and pork pies became particularly popular. Every county in England established its own particular flavouring for the pork filling, seasonings such as mace, pepper, ginger, coriander and nutmeg. The pork may be brined, in which case the filling is pink, or unbrined, when the filling will be grey. The hot pies are filled with gelatinous stock made from the trimmings and bones of the pig, which sets to a clear jelly as it cools.

A common variation on the pork pie is Gala pie – a pork pie with a hard-boiled egg in the centre. Gala pies are baked in long baking tins, with several eggs arranged along the centre of the meat.

Melton Mowbray in Leicestershire is home to what is probably the most famous pork pie in the world. A hand-raised case of rich, crisp, golden pastry encloses a filling of hand-chopped pork and tasty jelly. The area is also famous for its Stilton cheese, which has been made here since the eighteenth century. After making cheese, the surplus whey was fed to pigs and as a result, pig rearing increased. In the early nineteenth century, the town was also noted for its foxhunts, and pork pies were the perfect portable food for the hungry huntsmen. They took the tasty pies back to London, where their fame quickly spread and demand increased, so that the town's bakers had to step up production. Potteries also produced porcelain pork pies stamped with the town crest of Melton Mowbray for visitors to take home as souvenirs.

Every producer has their own secret recipe, but generally speaking, Melton Mowbray pork pies are filled with highly seasoned, coarsely chopped, uncured pork. The hot water crust pastry is hand-moulded around a wooden block called a 'dolly', which is removed before the filling is added. The pies are glazed with beaten egg yolk to give a shiny, golden finish and then baked unsupported. This baking process is crucial to an authentic Melton Mowbray pork pie. After baking, a stock made from pigs' feet and bones is poured through a hole in the top and left to set to a jelly.

The Melton Mowbray Pork Pie Association, a small group of authentic pork pie makers, have gained PGI status (see page 113) for genuine Melton Mowbray pork pies after a 10-year campaign. Melton Mowbray pies can now be made only in the traditional manner, to the time-honoured recipe, in the vicinity of the town of Melton Mowbray.

Pork pies remain among the best-loved English foods. One couple in West Yorkshire loved them so much that in 2005 they opted for a three-tier pork pie on their wedding day instead of the traditional wedding cake! The huge pie weighed 22.5 kg (50 lb) and took 24 hours to bake and assemble.

THE RECIPES

bath chaps

These are delicious and well worth making at home every so often. Some say it should consist of the entire pig's head rolled around the tongue with the cheeks as the protective layer of fat; others say only the cheek is used. Note that you need a cheek with its skin and fat, not just the small nuggets of flesh that are sold as pigs' cheeks for casseroles. Nowadays it is quite hard to get a large cheek, but it's worth looking. The flat-headed breeds of pig are not suitable. Saltpetre keeps the meat a nice pink colour, but it is hard to get hold of these days and is not really necessary, but use it if available.

SERVES 6–8

1 pig's cheek, boneless
  with skin and fat, or half
  a pig's jaw with the bone
  and tongue attached

FOR THE DRY SALTING
500 g/1 lb 2 oz coarse
  sea salt
2 tsp crushed black
  peppercorns
1 tbsp granulated sugar

FOR THE COLD PICKLING
2 litres/3¹/2 pints water
300 g/11 oz coarse sea salt
200 g/7 oz coarse brown
  or granulated sugar
¹/2 tsp saltpetre (optional)
2 bay leaves
3 juniper berries

For the dry salting, mix the salt, peppercorns and sugar together. Find a plastic tub into which the chap will fit. Sprinkle the base with some of the salt mix, then lay the pig's cheek in and sprinkle all over with the rest of the mix, making sure the chap is well coated. Cover with a cloth and leave for 2–3 days, turning after the first full day.

For the pickling, put all the ingredients into a large pan and bring to the boil, stiring to dissolve the salt and sugar, then leave until completely cold.

Immerse the chap in the cold liquid – it must be completely covered – and leave in a cool place for at least 4 days, stirring every day. You can leave it for up to 9 days, if you like.

Remove the chap from the liquid and soak in fresh water overnight.

To cook, put the chap in a large pan, cover with cold water and simmer gently, skimming off any skum, for 2 hours, or until the meat is falling off the bone. Leave in the liquid until cool enough to handle, then carefully cut off the skin, remove all bones and gristle and trim off excess fat. Wrap the chap in a double layer of clingfilm in a tapering cone shape, and chill overnight.

Warm through, slice and serve with broad beans or pease pudding (see page 137) and mashed potatoes. It's also delicious cold.

kidneys with mustard and mushrooms

This is a very good supper dish served on toast or with rice. You can make it more spicy with Worcestershire sauce or chillies, but it is real homely comfort food for a cold evening.

Serves 4

4 pigs' kidneys
1 tsp vegetable oil
2 tsp butter
1 small onion, peeled and chopped
150 g/5 oz mushrooms, sliced
100 ml/3½ fl oz double cream
2 tsp Dijon mustard
salt and pepper

Slice the kidneys in half horizontally and then each half vertically and remove as much as you can of the white core. Cut the kidneys into fork-size pieces.

Heat a large frying or sauté pan with the vegetable oil, then add 1 tsp of the butter. Season the kidneys with salt and pepper and, as the butter melts to a fizzle, place the kidneys in the pan, keeping them apart so they brown quickly all over – it takes about 5 minutes, there should be a little blood still showing. Remove them from the pan and set aside.

Add the remaining butter to the pan, stir in the onion and allow to soften. Add the mushrooms, increase the heat and cook quickly until soft. Pour in the cream, stir in the mustard and bring to the boil. Reduce the heat, return the kidneys to the pan and heat through, then check for seasoning and serve.

brawn

This has been an essential part of the pig slaughter for centuries. It is made from the meat of a pig's head, which is sometimes salted first. This is because with all the other things being made after the slaughter, salting kept the head preserved for a little longer until the brawn maker was ready to start. Modern breeds of pig have heads so big they won't fit in the average pot, but if you seek out a rare breed or use just half a head, then the results will be delicious. It's a very economical dish and presents very well, so is ideal for a party centrepiece and it is excellent with salad, mustard and toast or baked potatoes. Fresh herbs are optional and I like parsley, but sage is traditional. Other seasonings can be chilli, which gives it a spicy heat, grated lemon zest or lemon juice. Traditionally, it was also an opportunity to 'turn out' the spice box with bits of nutmeg or whatever. There are no hard and fast rules.

1 pig's head, split in half,
  or ¹/₂ a head – ask your
  butcher to saw rather
  than chop, to avoid bone
  splinters
1 bunch of fresh sage
  or parsley stalks
3 bay leaves
2 tsp black peppercorns
2 tsp sea salt
onion skins (only the
  golden skins, as the onion
  itself can make the stock
  ferment)
2 green chillies (optional),
  with seeds
plenty of chopped fresh
  parsley or sage or both
grated zest or juice of
  ¹/₂ lemon (optional)
salt and black pepper

Scrub the head, particularly around the ears, and remove any obvious bone splinters. Carefully pull out the brains and if you like, you can use the cheeks for chaps (see page 234).

Put the head into a large pan with the sage or parsley stalks, the bay leaves, peppercorns, sea salt, onion skins and chillies, if using them, and cover with water. Bring to the boil, then reduce the heat to a gentle simmer and skim off any froth or scum. Leave to cook, uncovered, for about 4 hours, or until the meat is falling from the bone. If you have a range cooker, such as an Aga, you can cook it overnight in the simmering oven. Top up with water if necessary, from time to time.

Once cooked, allow it to cool a little. Remove the meat, then strain the liquid through a fine sieve into a clean pan and boil rapidly to reduce (it may need to be skimmed again). Meanwhile, remove all the meat from the bones – this should be easy, as it will fall away. Discard the bones, and eyeballs, peel the tongue and discard the rough skin. Roughly chop the meat – and as much of the skin and fat as you want to include – and season with salt and black pepper. When the stock has well reduced, probably by about half, blanch the chopped parsley and/or sage in it – this prevents them spoiling. Mix the herbs and lemon zest or juice, if using, with the meat and pack the mixture into a pudding basin or terrine, then pour the hot stock on top to just cover. Leave to set in a cool place. The jelly will set solid.

When ready to serve, unmould by pouring hot water onto the base, or dipping it into hot water, and turn out – it will delight you with a quivering mass of multi-textured meats interspersed with flecks of green. Brawn will keep in the fridge for over 1 week, but won't freeze, as the jelly goes liquid.

Food for thought

Brains have a velvety, melt-in-the-mouth texture and delicate flavour and are highly prized in France and Italy; you won't see them for sale in the United Kingdom, but if you buy a pig's head to make brawn I recommend that you gently pull out the brains and try this simple way of cooking them: think of it as the chef's perk.

Soak them in cold water for 1–2 hours, changing the water once or twice. Poach them in gently simmering water – with a slice of onion or shallot and a bay leaf – for about 15 minutes. Pat them dry on kitchen paper, then cut into two or three pieces and roll in seasoned flour.

Heat a tablespoon each of olive oil and butter in a small pan and when the butter foams, add the brains. Cook over medium heat for 3–4 minutes, turning them gently, until crisp and golden brown. Drain on kitchen paper and eat while they are hot, with a little squeeze of lemon juice.

faggots

My mother-in-law remembers her mother making these from the slaughtered family pig and she has passed on the recipe. My research has shown that these are also popular in the north of England, where bog myrtle was often used to season them. You will need caul fat — the thin membrane of fat that encircles the gut in the pig (see page 215). Ask your butcher.

Serves up to 10

900 g/2 lb pork belly
900 g/2 lb streaky bacon
1 pig's heart
250 g/9 oz pig's liver
$^1/_4$ tsp ground nutmeg
 and ginger
$^1/_2$ tsp black pepper
2 tsp chopped fresh sage,
 marjoram, thyme and bog
 myrtle, if you can find it
1 onion, peeled and
 chopped
550 g/1$^1/_4$ lb fresh brown
 breadcrumbs
3 large eggs, lightly beaten
1 pig's caul
a little pork or chicken
 stock

Chop the meats together and then add the seasonings and onion. Pass through a mincer set to a coarse mince. Mix in the breadcrumbs and bind with the eggs. Form into small balls.

Preheat the oven to 190°C/375°F/gas 5.

Soften the caul in water, then spread it out and cut into squares large enough to enclose each meatball. Wrap the caul around the faggots. Place them in a roasting tray, add a little stock to prevent them from drying out, then cook in the oven for about 1 hour.

BUTTERY ROWIES

MAKES 16

½ tbsp dried yeast
1 tbsp soft brown sugar
350 ml/12 fl oz warm water
500 g/1 lb 2 oz strong
 white flour
a pinch of salt
200 g/7 oz butter
100 g/3½ oz lard

The traditional Aberdonian breakfast roll. The method is similar to that for making a croissant, but I think these are much more delicious. I once stayed up all night at a party and next morning made a batch of these wonderful pastries. Hangovers were cleared very quickly as the smell of freshly baked butteries wafted over the sleeping partygoers!

Mix the yeast with the sugar and a little of the warm water to dissolve the yeast, then set aside in a warm place for about 10 minutes, until the yeast is frothy. Mix the flour with the salt in a large bowl. When the yeast has bubbled up, pour it into the flour with the rest of the water. Mix well and knead to form a smooth dough, then cover with a clean cloth and leave in a warm place to rise until doubled in size, about 1 hour.

Cream the butter and lard together and divide into three. The mixture should be soft enough to spread easily but not melting.

When the dough has doubled in size, knock it back (this means knead it again until the dough is back to its normal size), and then roll it out to a rectangle about 1 cm/½ inch thick. Spread a third of the butter mixture over two-thirds of the dough. Fold the other third of the dough over onto the butter, then fold the other third over, giving three layers. Press the edges together firmly. Roll out to the original size and fold into thirds as before – this time without a layer of fat, then leave to rest in a cool place for at least 40 minutes. Repeat the above procedure, including leaving to rest, twice more, to finish the butter mixture.

Roll out the dough to a rectangle about 1 cm/½inch thick. Cut the dough into 16 squares. Shape into rough circles by folding the edges in all the way around, then place on a baking sheet. Leave to rise, covered with a dry cloth, for 45 minutes.

Preheat the oven to 200°C/400°F/gas 6. Bake for 15 minutes until golden-brown and flaky. Serve with butter and marmalade or raspberry jam.

THE BIG BREAKFAST

The classic British breakfast includes a surprisingly large amount of pig bits: bacon, sausage, black pudding and kidneys, with the sausage and black puddings varying from region to region. It's actually not the easiest of meals to prepare, as there are so many elements that need to be just right. You can start with a buck's fizz, followed by a plate of porridge and then perhaps into the meat. The devilled kidneys also make a supper dish on their own.

Turn the oven on low so you can keep everything warm prior to assembly for serving – I find a roasting tray is perfect for the job.

sausages

I defer to Nigel Slater for the sausages; they need to be cooked slowly and he always cooks them in a pan over a low heat with a little lard to start them off. He then cooks them, covered with a lid, for 30–40 minutes. The result is a very sticky, dark, succulent sausage, but they do need to be good sausages to start with, with a decent quantity of fat.

Another way of cooking them is under the grill, but make sure you cook them before the bacon and lower the grill pan so the heat is not so direct as for bacon. If you cook them in this way, you will probably be eating less fat. Transfer to the roasting tray and keep warm in the oven.

black pudding

These usually come as a long cylinder and can be sliced and grilled like a sausage, first perhaps nicking the plastic casing so it comes off easily after cooking. Grill on one side for 5 minutes, then turn and cook the other side for about 3 minutes. The smaller, rounded black puddings can be cooked whole and are best cooked in a medium oven (190°C/375°F/gas 5) for 10 minutes. Transfer to the roasting tray and keep warm in the oven.

bacon

Whatever type, style or cut you choose, bacon is usually best grilled to allow it to lose any excess fat. Make sure the grill is hot before you start and place the rashers on the grill so they are not overlapping. Cook for 3–4 minutes, then turn them over to cook the other side. Transfer to the roasting tray and keep warm in the oven.

Assemble the breakfast and enjoy!

devilled kidneys

Sweat the onion in the butter until soft, then stir in the mustard. Add the kidneys and seal over a high heat, then reduce the heat, cover the pan and cook slowly for 4 minutes.

Remove the lid, increase the heat, season and pour in the brandy – if you have a gas flame, let it catch light; if not, just allow it to bubble. Serve hot, with chopped parsley.

SERVES 4

½ onion, peeled and chopped
25 g/1 oz butter
½ tsp Dijon mustard
2 pig's kidneys, cut into quarters, skin and core removed
salt and pepper
1 tbsp brandy
chopped fresh parsley
to serve

French toast

MAKES 6 SLICES

3 eggs
1 tbsp milk
salt
300 g/11 oz butter
6 slices white bread
marmalade to serve,
optional

Beat the eggs with the milk and a little salt in a large bowl. Melt some of the butter in a pan. While the pan is heating, dip the bread into the egg mixture, making sure it is well coated. Hold it briefly above the bowl to allow excess egg to drip off, then place the slice into the hot pan. Cook as many slices as you like, but do not overcrowd the pan. After 3 or so minutes, the side touching the pan should be golden; turn the bread over and brown the other side. Remove and keep warm. Continue to cook slices adding butter as necessary. Spread with marmalade and serve.

pig's liver with lemon and honey

This is based on an idea from my mother and requires all the ingredients to be prepared before you start cooking since it is so quick to make. Some people like to soak the liver in milk prior to cooking, as this helps to soften the strong flavour that liver sometimes has. Make sure the strips are of a similar thickness so they all cook at the same time.

Serves 2–4

450 g/1 lb pig's liver,
  trimmed and cut into
  thin strips
2 tbsp plain flour, seasoned
  with salt and pepper
2 tsp vegetable oil
25 g/1 oz butter
the juice of 1 lemon
1 tbsp honey

Heat a heavy-based pan. Toss the liver in the seasoned flour and shake off the excess. Add the oil and butter to the pan, then, as the butter melts and foams up, quickly cook the liver to colour on all sides. Remove and keep warm.

Pour off any excess fat from the pan, then add the lemon juice and honey. They will bubble up. Return the liver to the pan, turn to coat it in the sauce, then serve immediately with rice and a salad.

CASSOULET

One cannot have a book about cooking pig in all its forms without a recipe for cassoulet. As soon as one enters the arena of this great dish, purists from all quarters will circle, looking for mistakes. Cassoulet is a regional French dish from the Languedoc, and is cooked all over the region, from Carcassonne to Toulouse, with Castelnaudary somewhere in the middle, and inevitably there are local variations – which type of beans, whether to include only pork products, or also mutton, preserved goose or duck. It is really down to flavour – and the quality of the stock and the long, slow cooking brings this out.

I have decided to supply two recipes. One is based on the traditional method, including lamb or, better still, mutton, but not preserved goose or duck, as I feel that the texture is lost in the whole. The other is a simplified version, and that's where we begin...

cheat's cassoulet

This recipe is about looking to use what you have to hand. The duck legs can be replaced by pheasant or other game birds (you may use the breasts for a different dish), and you can substitute the pork belly with diced shoulder of pork, or you could use lamb. The garlic sausage can be replaced with a bit of salami or maybe a sausage local to your area or just the end of a ham chopped into chunks – very often, the end bits add lots of flavour, even if you don't actually eat it but remove before serving.

SERVES 4

200 g/7 oz dried white
 beans
4 duck legs
400 g/14 oz pork belly
2 tbsp lard
1 large onion, peeled and
 chopped
2 carrots, peeled and diced
1 large leek, trimmed,
 diced and washed
3 garlic cloves, peeled
 and pulped
1 bay leaf
800 g/1lb 12 oz canned
 tomatoes
1 tsp tomato purée
200 g/7 oz cured garlic
 sausage
salt and pepper
chopped parsley to serve

You need to start this the day before – better still, make it two days ahead and reheat for 20–30 minutes before serving. Thoroughly rinse the beans in cold water, checking for small stones. Soak them overnight in cold water.

The next day, preheat the oven to 230°C/450°F/gas 8.

Drain the beans and place in a pan with fresh cold water to cover, then bring to the boil, reduce the heat and simmer for 30 minutes.

Meanwhile, season the duck legs and pork belly with salt and pepper, place in a roasting tin with the lard and roast in the oven for 30 minutes, basting twice. Place in a casserole. Drain the beans and place on top of the meat.

Brown the onion, carrots and leek in the fat from the roasted meats: you can do this by putting them in the roasting tin used for the meats and returning it to the hot oven for 10 minutes, or by pouring the fat from the meats into a frying pan and browning them in that. Add them to the casserole with the garlic, bay leaf, tomatoes, tomato purée and garlic sausage, then add just enough water to cover. Cover with a lid and bring to the boil. Reduce the oven temperature to 190°C/375°F/gas 5. Place the casserole in the oven and cook for 3 hours, turning occasionally and making sure it doesn't dry out – add a little hot stock if necessary.

When cooked, remove the pork belly and the sausage and cut into chunks. Return them to the pan and reheat on a simmer to achieve the correct texture – a sort of coating sauce. Sprinkle liberally with chopped parsley.

traditional cassoulet

Traditionally, nothing is served before a cassoulet, but serve a green salad with it, and lots of crusty bread. You need to start this the day before you want to eat it. As with the cheats cassoulet, you can replace the garlic sausage with a bit of salami or other sausage.

SERVES 4–6

450 g/1 lb dried white haricot beans

FOR THE STOCK
1.5 kg/3 lb 5 oz lamb bones
3 tbsp tomato purée
2 litres/3½ pints hot pork or chicken stock (see page 259)
fresh bouquet garni (see page 274)
350 ml/12 fl oz dry white wine

FOR THE MEAT
450 g/1 lb boneless lamb or mutton taken from the leg
450 g/1 lb pork shoulder

1 tbsp flour, seasoned with salt and pepper
3–4 tbsp goose fat or lard
1 or 2 pig's trotters (optional)
2 onions, peeled and chopped
2 carrots, peeled and diced
12 garlic cloves, peeled – 10 pulped,
 2 cut into thin slices
fresh bouquet garni (see page 274)
115 g/4 oz petit salé (see page 197) or thick,
 unsmoked, bacon rashers
400 g/14 oz garlic sausage
400 g/14 oz canned chopped tomatoes
salt and pepper

First make the stock. Preheat the oven to 230°C/450°F/gas 8. Mix the bones and tomato purée together in a roasting tin and roast in the oven for 45 minutes, turning occasionally to get an even brown colour. Transfer the bones to a stock pot and add the hot stock and bouquet garni. Put the roasting tin on the hob, pour in some of the wine and allow to bubble up, then using a spoon or spatula, deglaze the tin by scraping up all the bits left on the bottom. Pour into the stock pot along with the rest of the wine and top up with water, if necessary, to just cover the bones. Bring to the boil and skim off any grease and debris, then reduce the heat and allow the stock to simmer for a couple of hours. Leave to cool overnight.

Thoroughly rinse the beans in cold water, checking for small stones. Soak them overnight in cold water.

The day has arrived (but you may decide to make the cassoulet the day before you want to serve it). Skim off the fat from the stock made the previous day and strain the stock, discarding the bones and herbs.

Dice the lamb or mutton and the pork into 4cm/1½ inch cubes and dust in the seasoned flour. Heat 1 tbsp of the goose fat or lard in a large sauté pan over a medium high heat and brown the cubes quickly. Don't crowd the pan or else the meat will not brown, so do it in batches. Place the browned meat in a large casserole.

Dust the trotters in the seasoned flour and brown them as well. Add to the casserole.

Lightly brown the onions and carrots in the sauté pan, adding more fat if necessary, and then just at the last minute add the pulped garlic, taking care not to burn it. Scrape all the vegetables into the casserole, then deglaze the sauté pan with a little of the strained stock to scrape up the residue. Drain the beans and add to the casserole with the rest of the stock and the bouquet garni. Bring to the boil, pushing the bouquet garni under the surface of the liquid. Reduce the heat and allow to simmer very gently for 1½ hours, or until the meat is tender. Simmering is very important – don't allow to boil, as the meat may toughen.

Once cooked, strain off the stock into a large bowl and leave to cool, then degrease. Remove the herbs and return the lamb, pork, beans and vegetables to the casserole. When cool enough to handle, remove the pig's trotters and discard the fatty skin and bones, then return the chunks of meat to the casserole.

Bring a pan of water to the boil. Cut the bacon into lardons (see page 87), then blanch in the water for 2 minutes. Drain and refresh in cold water, then add to the casserole. Add the garlic sausage and chopped tomatoes to the casserole, stirring in gently so as not to break up the beans and meat.

Add the sliced garlic, then pour on just enough reserved stock to cover. Simmer gently for another hour, topping up the stock as necessary to prevent it drying out. What you are trying to create is a medium thick sauce around beans and meat, neither pea purée-thick nor soup-thin!

Take the sausage out, cut into 1 cm/½ inch slices and return to the casserole. Season to taste with salt and pepper. Take the whole dish to the table and serve in large bowls.

Castillian pig's trotters

The French don't have a monopoly on pigs' trotters and here is a Spanish dish, harking back to the days of the Moorish empire.

SERVES 4

4 trotters, preferably
  from the front legs,
  split lengthways
1 onion, peeled and
  stuck with 4 cloves
1 garlic clove, peeled
2 carrots, peeled and
  chopped
3 bay leaves
1 tbsp lard
1 onion, peeled and
  chopped finely
1 garlic clove, finely chopped
1 tbsp almonds, roughly
  chopped
1 tbsp flour
125 ml/4 fl oz dry white wine
1 tsp hot paprika
salt and pepper

Wash the trotters thoroughly, then place in a pan with the whole onion, garlic, carrots and 1 bay leaf. Cover with water and bring to the boil, then season with salt and pepper. Skim off any skum, then cover and simmer for 2–3 hours, or until the meat is almost falling from the bone. Lift the trotters out and set aside, covered with foil. Strain the cooking liquid and reserve.

Heat the lard in another pan and sweat the chopped onion and garlic over a gentle heat, until soft. Stir in the almonds and flour and cook until coloured slightly. Add the wine and 500 ml/18 fl oz of the strained cooking liquid, stirring all the time to prevent lumps. Add the remaining 2 bay leaves and season with the paprika, salt and pepper to taste, then simmer for 10 minutes.

Add the trotters to the pan, then gently simmer for 20 minutes. Serve with rice or noodles. This is also good left overnight and reheated.

SERVES 4

4 pigs' trotters, preferably
  from the front legs,
  washed thoroughly and
  tied in pairs heel to toe
200 ml/7 fl oz white wine
200 ml/7 fl oz wine vinegar
6 cloves
2 bay leaves
1 sprig of marjoram
4 tsp sugar
2 tsp salt
  tsp ginger
2 garlic cloves, peeled and
  crushed
fresh breadcrumbs
salt and pepper

Place the trotters in an ovenproof pan with a lid.

Add all the remaining ingredients except the breadcrumbs and top up with water to just cover. Bring to the boil, skim off any scum, then cover and simmer very gently for 8 hours, topping up with water as necessary. You can also cook them in a slow oven (140°C/275°F/gas 1) for the same time.

When cooked, leave to cool slightly, then place a plate on top to press the trotters close together so when they cool they keep their shape. Leave to cool completely. They will set in a wonderful jelly.

Remove them from the jelly, remove the string and carefully separate them. Sprinkle with breadcrumbs and then, to heat them through, either microwave on full power for a couple of minutes (Mathieu's method) or put into a medium oven (190°C/375°F/gas 5) for 30 minutes, and then brown quickly under a hot grill. Meanwhile, reheat the jelly until it is liquid, strain through a fine sieve. Serve the trotters with a little of the strained boiled juices.

Either that or go to the Hotel Le Cheval Rouge at Ste Menéhould.

pied de cochon Ste Menéhould

This is a rather special recipe for me as, of course, eagle-eyed readers will have spotted that my surname is the same as the word for a pig's foot. I first ate pigs' trotters when I went to work in the Hotel Anthon in Obersteinbach, in the Alsace region of France. On my way there, I stayed the night at the hotel in the town of Ste Menéhould. There I found the local speciality was this dish. It was delicious and you could eat the whole thing, bones and all. Thirty years later, I returned with my son on a trip and we stayed in the same hotel where current chef Mathieu Fourreau is still preparing the same dish. He was good enough to share the recipe with me — the secret is in the vinegar. This helps to break down the bones in the trotters so you can eat everything, and the luscious meat makes a rich accompanying sauce.

pork pie

The most British of all pies, the best-known area for which is Melton Mowbray (see page 231). The distinctive pink look of the filling comes from the anchovy essence. The traditional Melton Mowbray pie is 'raised' by hand with no mould: this takes expertise, which comes with practice. For your first attempt, use a springform cake tin. You can also buy special hinged pie cases, which unclip once the pie is cooked. It is important to give yourself time to prepare this dish, but it is worth the work. Knuckle of veal is sometimes hard to find, but using split trotters gives a good jellied stock.

SERVES 10-12

1 kg/2½ lb pork shoulder
225 g/8 oz gammon or ham
1 tsp each of salt and
  ground white pepper
4 sage leaves and sprigs
  of marjoram, finely
  chopped

FOR THE STOCK/JELLY
2 pig's trotters, split
1 knuckle of veal
  (optional)
pig's ears and tail
  (optional)
fresh bouquet garni: sprigs
  of sage, marjoram and
  parsley and 1 bay leaf
1 onion, peeled and stuck
  with 5 cloves
1 tbsp anchovy essence

FOR THE CRUST
600 g/1 lb 5 oz plain flour
½ tsp salt
250 g/9 oz lard
200 ml/7 fl oz water
1 egg, beaten

It's best if you can start the day before. Make sure the pork shoulder is free from gristle and then cut it into 1–2 cm/1½–¾ inch dice. Mince the ham, add to the pork with the salt and pepper and herbs and mix well. It's best to leave this overnight to allow the flavours to develop.

Make the stock/jelly (this can be done the day before). Put all the ingredients except the anchovy essence into a large pot and cover with cold water. Bring to the boil, skim off any froth or scum and then simmer gently for about 3 hours. Strain through a colander, then return the liquid to the stove and boil to reduce to about 600 ml/1 pint. Add the anchovy essence, then strain though a fine sieve to remove any remaining solids.

For the crust, place the flour and salt in a deep bowl and make a well in the middle. Bring the lard and water to the boil in a pan and then pour into the well, stirring with a wooden spoon. Mix until it forms a smooth paste, then work it well for a few minutes. Leave to rest in a warm place for about 15 minutes.

Preheat the oven to 200°C/400°F/gas 6. Line the base and sides of a springform cake tin with oiled greaseproof paper.

Take two-thirds of the dough and roll out to about 1 cm/½ inch thick. Use to line the cake tin, pressing the dough into the bottom and up the sides of the tin. Place the meat mixture inside, filling closely but not too forcefully. Roll out the remaining third of the dough for a lid, create a small hole in the middle and place on top of the filling. Press the edges to seal, then brush over with beaten egg and bake for 30 minutes. Reduce the oven temperature to 160°C/325°F/gas 3 and bake for a further 1½–2 hours, or until the juices run clear – test with a skewer through the hole in the centre of the pie.

When the pie is cooked, allow it to sit for 15–20 minutes, then carefully remove the side of the springform tin and the greaseproof paper. Brush the sides of the pan with the beaten egg and return to the oven for 15 minutes to glaze the outside. Leave the pie to cool for about 1 hour – it will still be slightly warm. Gently reheat the stock/jelly. Pour the stock into a jug, and then use a funnel to pour it into the hole in the middle of the pie until it just comes to the top. Leave to set and then chill.

pork scratchings

Apart from the oink, there really is nothing we throw away of the pig. Even the skin – if it's not gloriously crunchy as crackling or as melty in a slow-cooked shoulder – has the salty, crunchy, I-need-a-drink taste and texture of scratchings when cooked like this. This can be made in two ways (I am sure there are others, but these are the two I like) – it's all down to salting to remove moisture and then cooking to remove fat and create crunch. The skin from a 1.5–2 kg/3–4¹/₂ lb piece of pork loin will make enough scratchings for 8 people.

SERVES 8

pork skin (from a
  1.5–2 kg/3–4¹/₂ lb
  piece of pork loin)
fine sea salt

Sprinkle the skin all over with salt. Then cut into 2 cm/¾ inch wide strips. Place on a rack over a tray and leave in a cool place for 24–48 hours.

Now, this is where you have a choice of frying or roasting.

Frying

Dry the pieces of skin – by now, they will have exuded a little moisture. Heat vegetable oil in a deep-fryer or a pan to 170°C/340°F (test by frying a small cube of bread: it should brown in 40 seconds). Add the pieces of skin and fry until the crisp up. Drain on kitchen paper and serve, sprinkled with a little sea salt.

Roasting

Dry as above, then roast in a hot oven (240°C/475°F/gas 9) for 30 minutes, then reduce the temperature to 160°C/325°F/gas 3 and cook until they are golden brown and crunchy – this may take another 40 minutes.

stock

Possibly the most important base for all cooking, a good stock can make a great soup, or be the foundation for a sauce, stew or casserole. Without it, there would be no grand European cuisine. All the cooking-in-the-pot dishes in this book are based on the flavours coming from bones and slow-cooked vegetables.

You need to have bones – the butcher always has spare ones, but you may need to ask in advance. Ask him to chop them up quite small to give more of a surface area for colour and flavour. Loin bones and knuckle are best, but it's important to get the knuckle bones cut small, as it's not easy to do this at home. A pig's trotter also makes great stock and will add body because of its gelatinous juices. You need to gauge the amount of bones to fit into your largest pan. The amount below will fit into a big roasting tin. After stock made with a roast chicken carcass, pork stock, for me, is the easiest to make.

MAKES ABOUT
1 LITRE/1³/₄ PINTS

1 kg/2¹/₄ lb pork bones, chopped into small pieces
1 pig's trotter, split (optional)
2 onions, peeled, with skins reserved, and chopped
2 carrots, peeled and chopped
2 sticks of celery, chopped
parsley stalks
1 sprig of thyme
1 bay leaf

Preheat the oven to its highest setting. Place the pork bones and trotter, if you have it, in a roasting tin and brown in the oven for 15 minutes, turning the pieces once or twice to colour all over. Transfer the bones and trotter to a large pan; reserve the fat that has come from them in the tin. Roughly strew the vegetables into the roasting tin and coat with the fat. Brown them in the hot oven for about 15 minutes.

Meanwhile, cover the bones in the pan with cold water and bring slowly to simmering point. Skim off any scum from time to time. Add the herbs and the browned vegetables along with the onion skins. Simmer, skimming occasionally, for about 4 hours.

Leave to cool slightly, then strain through a sieve and leave until cold. Once it is cold, you can remove the fat from the surface. The resulting golden liquid will keep in the fridge for up to 1 week or it can be frozen.

To use, boil to reduce it and intensify the flavour if needed. Note there is no salt and pepper – add your own at the appropriate moment in a dish.

tomato sauce

Dangerous territory indeed! Every cook has his or her own tomato sauce recipe, and this is mine. It has developed over the years from my days in the kitchens of the Savoy hotel, London, whose original chef was Auguste Escoffier and who, it is argued by none other than the great food writer Elizabeth David, invented the idea of canning tomatoes. So I like to think that the spirit of the great French chef lives on in this sauce. You can use fresh tomatoes if you can get really ripe ones, or canned ones will do.

**MAKES ABOUT
850 ML/1½ PINTS**

2 tbsp olive oil
1 large onion, peeled
  and chopped
1 stick of celery, chopped
1 carrot, peeled and
  chopped
1 kg/2¼ lb fresh ripe
tomatoes, roughly
chopped, or 800 g/
1lb 12 oz canned
chopped plum tomatoes
1 garlic clove, peeled and
  crushed
1 bay leaf
1 sprig of thyme
1 strip of orange peel
salt and pepper

Heat the olive oil in a heavy-based pan, then gently cook the onion, celery and carrot until soft but not coloured, about 15 minutes.

Add the tomatoes plus a can full of water, or 125 ml/4 fl oz water if cooking fresh tomatoes. Reduce the heat to a very gentle simmer, add the garlic, herbs, orange peel and seasoning and cook very gently for 30 minutes, adding a little more water if it seems to be getting dry.

You can either push this sauce through a sieve or liquidise it first and then sieve it, which makes sieving easier. But it must be sieved to remove the pips and herby bits. This will keep, covered, in the fridge for a week.

Madeira sauce

Here is a classic sauce that goes well with a boiled ham. You can use either stock (on page 259) or the liquid in which you have cooked the ham, as long as it's not too salty.

MAKES 300 ML/10 FL. OZ

1 tbsp butter

4 shallots, peeled and finely chopped

2 small carrots, peeled and finely chopped

2 tsp flour

6 tbsp Madeira

1 tsp tomato purée

600 ml/1 pint hot stock (see page 259)

salt and pepper

Melt 2 tsp of the butter in a small saucepan, add the shallots and carrots and cook until lightly browned. Add the flour and stir-fry for a few minutes. Add 4 tbsp of the Madeira and the tomato purée and stir until the mixture dries. Stir in the hot stock and bring to the boil, then skim off any scum from the surface and cook until reduced by half.

At the last minute, add the rest of the Madeira and beat in a knob of cold butter. At this point, don't allow the sauce to boil again. Check for seasoning, strain and serve.

sauce gribiche

This is a great accompaniment to cold ham and other cold cuts, such as brawn or chap (see pages 238 and 234). It possibly dates back to Roman times and it's a sort of mayonnaise without the raw egg emulsion. When I worked at the Connaught Hotel in London, under the great chef Michel Bourdin, he had an hors d'oeuvre section that always had the sauce available since guests would ask for it with the oddest things.

MAKES ABOUT
300 ML/10 FL OZ

1 tbsp Dijon mustard
2 tbsp tarragon vinegar
250 ml/9 fl oz warm
  groundnut oil
2 tbsp capers, squeezed
  dry and roughly chopped
2 tsp chopped fresh
  tarragon leaves
1 tsp chopped fresh parsley
the yolks only of 5
  hard-boiled eggs,
  pushed through a sieve
salt and pepper

Put the mustard and vinegar with salt and pepper to taste into a blender and whiz to mix together, then with the motor running, gradually pour in the warm groundnut oil. Stop before you finish adding the oil, check for seasoning and if the mixture is very thick add a little warm water. It should be thinner than mayonnaise but still with some texture. Pour into a bowl, add the remaining ingredients and stir in. Check for seasoning and texture, adding more oil or water as necessary.

As with mayonnaise, it is important that the oil is warm, as this helps to create the liaison.

pastry

The pastry for raised pies is best made with lard, and I think that lard also makes a more flaky shortcrust pastry. You can use a mix of lard and butter, if you wish, but make sure you use half the weight of fat to flour.

500 g/1 lb 2 oz plain
 white flour
250 g/9 oz cold lard,
 cut into pieces
1 tsp salt

Place all the ingredients in a food processor and whiz until the mixture resembles fine breadcrumbs. Pour in about 6 tbsp cold water and continue to whiz until the dough forms a ball, adding more cold water as needed – do not overprocess. You can use straight away or wrap and leave in a cool place.

skirlie

Especially delicious with roast pork, this traditional Scottish side dish is also very good with roast game birds.

SERVES 4

50 g/2 oz butter
1 medium onion, peeled
 and finely chopped
125 g/4 oz medium oatmeal
salt and pepper

Melt the butter in a pan, add the onion and fry gently to soften and colour lightly. Stir in the oatmeal, season and allow to cook gently for 10 minutes.

lardy cake

My grandfather lived in Wiltshire and my aunt — his oldest daughter — lived with him to look after him into his old age. One of my family holidays from Scotland was to stay for a few weeks at my grandfather's with my mum to give my aunt a holiday. A highlight was to go to the local baker and buy an oozing lardy cake. We brought it home and warmed it in the oven and then only after we had eaten our sandwiches were we allowed a slice of rich, greasy cake. I remember the fat running down my lips and quickly working my tongue over my bottom lip so as not to lose any of it.

MAKES A 20 CM/8 INCH SQUARE CAKE

500 g/1 lb 2 oz white bread dough (see opposite)
175 g/6 oz cold lard, cut into small cubes
175 g/6 oz mixed dried fruit
50 g/2 oz mixed peel
175 g/6 oz caster sugar
a pinch of ground nutmeg, cinnamon or allspice

Roll out the dough into a large oblong, and dot the top two-thirds of it with one-third each of the lard, fruit, peel and sugar. Fold the dough into three, bringing the bottom third up, then folding it over again. Press the edges firmly with a rolling pin to seal and give the dough a quarter turn. Repeat twice more, adding the spice for the last roll. Roll out the dough to fit a greased 23 cm/9 inch diameter or 20 cm/8 inch square baking tin and leave in a warm place to rise for 30 minutes.

Preheat the oven to 190°C/375°F/gas 5. Bake the cake for about 45 minutes. While still hot from the oven, turn out of the tin upside down, onto a plate, and cut into sticky squares.

white bread

There's nothing more appetizing than the smell of freshly baked bread. Use it for a bacon or sausage sandwich or serve it with rillettes or pâté.

500 g/1 lb 2 oz strong
  white flour
2 tsp salt
2 tsp dried yeast
1 tsp brown sugar
275 ml/9½ fl oz warm
  water
1 tbsp vegetable oil

Put the flour in a large bowl with the salt and leave in a warm place.

Meanwhile, put the yeast, sugar and about half of the warm water into a jug. Stir well to dissolve the yeast. Leave in a warm place, with a cloth over the top, until the yeast begins to froth, about 10 minutes.

When the yeast is ready, pour onto the flour and mix in with the remaining warm water and the oil. Knead by hand or in a mixer with a dough hook. The texture should be smooth and moist, but it should not stick to your hands. Shape into a ball and place in a lightly oiled bowl, cover with a cloth and leave in a warm place to rise. The dough should double in size.

Knock back the dough and knead for a few minutes, then place in an oiled loaf tin (make sure you brush the oil into the corners of the tin) or on an oiled baking sheet. Cover with a cloth and leave for 30–40 minutes, until puffy.

Preheat the oven to 200°C/400°F/gas 6. Bake the bread until deep golden brown, about 20–30 minutes. To test if it is cooked, turn the loaf out onto a cooling rack and tap the base: if there is a hollow thud, then it's cooked; if not, return to the oven for another 5 minutes.

cooking the whole hog

'But I will place this carefully fed pig within the crackling oven; and, I pray, what nicer dish can e'er be given to man.'

Aeschylus, Ancient Greek poet, circa 525–456BC

It is not clear when man first ate roast pig, although there are lots of stories and legends associated with this momentous event. In Europe, it is believed the animal was originally spit-roasted using green twig spits over open fires. As society developed and eating became a ceremonial ritual, the roasting of a whole pig demonstrated abundance and prosperity. A young pig took less time to cook and was sure to be succulent and tender.

Suckling (or sucking) pig is a young pig that has fed only on its mother's milk and is slaughtered between the ages of two and six weeks. Its meat and fat have a sweeter, and more delicate flavour than that of a fully grown pig.

In Ancient Greece, a piglet was fattened on grape must before slaughter and *koiridion* (a suckling pig stuffed with herbs and roasted) was a dish reserved for special occasions. Ancient Romans usually marinated the piglet in olive oil, salt and spices (pepper and cumin were the favourite choice), or sometimes boned the suckling pig and stuffed it with a mixture of meats, poultry, vegetables or fruits and spices, before cooking it on a spit. The skin became golden and crisp as the pig cooked and, to prevent it from burning, was covered with papyrus until the pig was cooked through.

Sucking pigs stuffed with various combinations of meat, herbs and spices were an important part of the splendid medieval feasts. Royal cook to the French court, Taillevent (1310–1395) included in his *Le Viandier* cookbook of 1373 complex instructions for *pourcelet farci* – suckling pig stuffed with cheese, egg yolks, chopped roast pork, chestnuts and spices, which was sewn up, roasted and basted with vinegar, oil and salt as it cooked on a spit in front of the fire. The delicate skin needed constant basting to prevent it from blistering and burning.

In the seventeenth century, the skin was often pulled off the cooked piglet and a mixture of spices, breadcrumbs and sugar was applied to the fat, which cooked to a crisp coating.

An eighteenth-century Italian recipe suggested stuffing the piglet with fried eels, garlic, herbs and fennel seeds and basting it with oil and water as it cooked on a spit. A sauce of anchovy oil and pistachios accompanied the cooked meat.

In England, Charles Lamb, in his 'Dissertation Upon Roast Pig' (1822), held that 'in the entire realm of edible things, roast pig is the most delicate', while celebrated diarist Samuel Pepys wrote that 'there could be nothing better for the digestion and the spirit than pickled oysters, a young roasted pig and good, heavy ale'.

Mrs Beeton in her celebrated *Book of Household Management* (first published in a bound edition in 1861) gave instructions for preparing a sucking pig, declaring that it 'should not be more than three weeks old'. It was scalded, the hairs pulled out, the entrails removed, the ears and nostrils thoroughly washed and then the whole pig was washed in cold water and wiped dry. The feet were removed and the animal was ready to be stuffed, rubbed with butter or oil and roasted.

Every pig-eating culture still enjoys spit-roasted pigs, although they are usually reserved for celebratory feasts. The best-known Italian roast pig is *porchetta*: a boned, whole sucking pig is well seasoned with herbs and spices and spit-roasted for hours. It's classic festival food and often found at markets and fairs.

The Sardinian *porceddu* is traditionally cooked in a pit lined with aromatic herbs and covered with rocks. A fire is built upon the rocks, and when it has burned for many hours, the pig is set upon it and covered first with hot coals and then with myrtle branches and the earth is piled back on top. Bandits who once populated the more isolated parts of the island used this method. In another method, a fire is built with aromatic woods such as juniper, myrtle, olive and arbutus. The pig is fastened to a large stick that is pushed into the ground in front of the fire. Once the pig is cooked, it is covered with myrtle leaves and left for 30 minutes or so before carving.

The Spanish and Portuguese are very fond of sucking pig (*cochinillo* and *leitão* respectively). In Spain, *cochinillo* is a speciality of the provinces of Segovia and Avila. A sucking pig, as defined by the Spanish, has fed only on mother's milk, has never been allowed to run free and is no more than a month old. While suckling its young, the sow feeds on rye, oats, cabbage and potatoes. Sucking pigs are sold in butchers' shops and markets and are easily recognisable by their white, waxy skin. The piglet is cooked with liberal amounts of garlic and herbs and the fat under the skin melts into the tender, succulent meat as a result of the long, slow cooking. *Cochinillo asado*, a traditional Castilian meal, features a one-month-old piglet roasted in an earthenware dish.

In Portugal, roast sucking pig is known as *leitão assado* and is a particular speciality of Mealhada, a town in central Portugal, where the traditional accompaniments are a crisp green salad, orange slices and fried potatoes.

Spanferkel (spit-roasted sucking pig) is served at the Oktoberfest in Germany, where the word also refers to a feast featuring the pig. Throughout Eastern Europe, spit-roasted hog features at celebratory feasts and family occasions. In Georgia, roast sucking pig (*gochi*) is a popular New Year's dish: and the crisp ears are given to the most important guest at dinner.

In Poland, *prosie pieczone* (sucking pig) was the traditional centrepiece of the Easter (*swieconka*) table and was served at the banquets of the Polish nobility. The piglet was stuffed with herbs, brushed with oil or butter, had a raw potato put into its mouth and was then roasted; after cooking, the potato was removed and replaced with an apple. At Easter, a small painted Easter egg (*pisanka*) was put into the piglet's mouth.

In the Caribbean, a whole pig smeared with spices and cooked slowly over a fire made from fragrant allspice wood is known as 'jerked pork'. Jerk was originally a way of drying and preserving meat created by the Carib and Arawak Indians who inhabited the Caribbean islands before the arrival of the Spanish in the fifteenth century. They slow-cooked their meat with spices in order to preserve it and this method was later refined by the Maroons (former slaves brought to Jamaica from West Africa), who used peppers to liberally season wild boar before cooking it for hours over slow-burning pimento wood until succulent.

The term 'jerk' may be an English corruption of the word *charqui*, a Spanish term for dried meat. Another possibility is linked to the 'jerking', or poking, of the meat with a sharp object to produce holes, which were

then filled with the spice mixture. Whole pigs are the traditional meat to jerk, but chicken and seafood are now also popular. Everyone has their own unique family recipe for jerk, but there are three essential basic jerk ingredients: allspice, thyme and Scotch Bonnet chillies (extremely fiery and searingly hot, but it's just not jerk without the heat, although milder chillies can be used instead).

In Cuba, a whole pig is marinated in Seville orange juice and/or lime juice, salt, garlic and oregano and is traditionally served on New Year's Day. As in the Hawaiian *luau* (traditional Hawaiian feast), the pig is usually covered with banana leaves and cooked over a fire in a pit.

Pig roasts have long been traditional in the southern United States, and in recent decades hog roasts have become increasingly popular in the United Kingdom, at agricultural shows, large markets and special parties.

GETTING STARTED

HOW TO DO IT

I have had many experiences of cooking hogs – and not just the boned-out pieces, so loved by the Italians, but the whole beast. Whether you're cooking a suckling pig at 5–6kg/11–13lb or an 80kg/176lb large beast to feed in excess of 150 people, it's a popular tradition the world over. A whole roast pig makes a great centrepiece to any celebration, but it does require thought and preparation. Here are a few tips on how to set about doing it.

The pig

In terms of price, finding a supplier to fit your budget can be difficult. If you want to buy a suckling pig, for example, piglets put on a lot of weight very quickly and they can double their weight within weeks, and so if a farmer is selling a small suckling pig he will be looking to get the same amount of money for it as he would for a larger one. Be prepared, therefore, to pay a premium price. Also, make sure you understand what the farmer or producer means by a 'suckling pig' – you want one that is still on its mother's milk and which weighs a maximum of 9kg/20lb. Otherwise larger ones will come down in price proportionally.

The equipment

The easiest solution is to hire an electric spit roast with a gas burner. There are plenty of companies now who will deliver to your door a machine complete with pig, ready to go. Use their instructions and you cannot go wrong, but do be sure that the pig is of a quality you want. Some suppliers of machines may buy a factory-reared animal, which will not be as flavoursome as a rare breed. Make sure you ask what you are getting.

For a smaller hog it's fun to create your own fire pit and it is possible to buy either a manual spit, which you place beside the fire pit and turn by hand, or one powered by electricity. In either case, be prepared for standing around for a long time!

Preparation

The electric spit roast with gas burner presents no problem – just plug it in, fire it up and forget about it. If you want to dig a fire pit, which will produce a better flavour in the meat, the pit should be longer than the pig to be cooked and wide enough to ensure a constant, even heat under the whole pig. You also need to make sure that any spit you make or buy is long enough to comfortably fit the whole pig on to, as the head needs careful cooking too. Some people consider the charred ears a real treat.

Dig your pit about 15cm/6in deep into the ground, making sure it is longer than the pig and about 60cm/24in wide. Build a large fire with good seasoned, dry wood. Once the fire has died down a little and is just hot, place your pig on the spit, making sure that you have carefully trussed the meat and turn the spit on. Cooking is all about look and feel. If the pig is spitting or colouring, then it's cooking, but it is safest to have a couple of thermometers to hand. You want to keep the temperature of the heat from the fire under the cooking pig at about 120°C/250°F. The temperature of the meat when it's cooked should be just above 63°C/145°F at the deepest part of the animal – use a meat thermometer for this: plunge it into the haunch or shoulder by the bone and leave it for a few minutes to register.

The fire, if built with sound wood, will keep a good heat for up to 2 hours. If you feel the need to top it up, add pieces of wood gently so as not to encourage big flames, as this can scorch the piglet.

As regards the preparation of the animal, if you have hired a machine, then just follow the instructions that come with it. You could put the animal in a brine or marinade, but I tend to feel that if you have bought a good rare breed animal, then all it needs is a little preparation the night before you intend to cook it: using a sharp knife such as a Stanley knife, score the pig heavily all over, from the back down to the belly and on the legs and shoulders. Make the cuts about 2cm/¾in apart, then rub in coarse salt and wine vinegar. The next day, just before cooking, brush off any excess salt.

Trussing

As the pig cooks, the meat loosens and shifts which could result in the meat falling off the spit, so it needs to be trussed (tied) to be held together. The spit should go between the thighs, along the inside of the body (just underneath the spine) and out through the mouth. The head, shoulders and legs should be trussed securely using kitchen twine, holding them against each other on the spit. Any excess kitchen twine should be removed to prevent it from burning.

Cooking times

Cooking times will vary depending on the temperature of the flame and the distance of the spit roast from the flame. There are no hard and fast rules. Generally, allow 1 hour for the fire to get hot before you start roasting the pork, then approximately 15–20 minutes per lb/½kg. So, for a 5–6kg/11–13lb hog which should comfortably serve 6–8 people, allow 3½–4½ hours cooking time.

Serving

The resting process is important with a whole pig. Once it is cooked, the pig will keep hot for a while, so don't attempt to eat anything until half an hour after you are happy it is cooked and it has had time to rest.

You can cut the meat directly from the animal on the spit, but you may feel safer placing the cooked pig on a tray or board and carving it in a safe environment. The meat will come easily off the bone. Start with the loin and move on to the legs and shoulder.

glossary of terms

Bain marie Also known as a water bath, this consists of a bowl or pan inside a pan or roasting tin filled with hot water to maintain a good temperature without boiling.

Beurre manié Soften an equal amount of butter with plain flour and use to thicken liquids by whisking the resulting paste into them, and then simmering for a few minutes.

Blanche Plunge into boiling water and then refresh in ice cold water until completely cold.

Deglaze Add a splash of wine or other alcohol to a pan in which a piece of meat has been cooked. This removes the 'glaze' from the cooking and you can then combine the resulting liquid into a sauce.

Degreasing stock The best way is first to allow the stock to cool. Next refrigerate it, and then you will be able to lift off the fat.

Egg wash An egg beaten with a little milk for use on pastry; make sure it's well beaten and is smooth without lumps. Use a decent size bowl.

Fresh bouquet garni This is a small packet of fresh herbs tied with string, used in stews and marinades. Once used, it can be easily discarded, as the packet keeps all the small bits – like peppercorns – together. To make, take 2 sticks of celery cut to about 8 cm/3¼ in. Put one stick in the packet, a bay leaf, a sprig of thyme, a parsley stalk and 6 peppercorns, then tie up the pack to the other stick of celery so that none of the ingredients can come out. Some people tie the other end of the string to the handle of the pan for ease of finding.

How to pulp garlic Peel the clove of garlic and place on the corner of a chopping board, sprinkle a small amount of salt over it and, using the back of a large knife, crush the garlic to break it up. Then, using the edge of the knife, pulverise the garlic with the salt. The salt helps to break down the fabric of the garlic and creates a pulp, thus using all of the garlic and wasting none. It's good either to use the edge of your board or to have a board especially for garlic and onions, as the flavour can linger.

Lardons Small strips of bacon; these can be bought or you can cut thick slices of bacon into 2 cm/¾ in lengths.

Lemon zest The skin of a lemon. To use as little of the white as possible, use a peeler to remove.

Salt The best is a coarse sea salt, but an ordinary salt will do.

Seasoned flour Plain flour which has had the addition of salt and pepper, to season meats as they are coated in flour for frying.

Seasoned milk Take the amount of milk you need and add a small peeled onion stuck with a couple of cloves and a bay leaf. Heat until just below boiling, then leave to infuse for 10 minutes, strain and discard the onion and bay leaf.

Quatre épices Is a classic French spice mix for pâté and terrines consisting of 125 g/4½ oz black pepper, 10 g/¼ oz cloves, 35 g/1¼oz nutmeg, 30 g/1 oz ginger. All ingredients are ground and mixed together.

index

A

accompaniments 35
  see also dressings for salads; sauces
ale
  casserole of pork with fresh herbs
    and ale 68–69
  to cook a ham in comfort 126
  honey pork with roast potatoes
    and apples 40
  pork with plums 70
allspice
  bigos 201
  cinghiale in dolce-forte 62–63
  country pâté 205
  fricadeller 202
  lardy cake 264
  pork and pistachio terrine 206
almonds
  Castillian pig's trotters 253
anchovy essence
  pork pies 256–257
apples
  baked chops in foil with apple
    and honey 75
  choucroute garni 196
  to cook a ham in comfort 126
  honey pork with roast potatoes
    and apples 40
  roast rolled leg of pork with sesame
    potatoes & wild garlic apple sauce 39
  sausage, apple & beetroot
    sandwiches 179
asparagus
  ham with asparagus and

Hollandaise 136
Asturian bean stew 95
aubergines
  sausage, aubergine & courgette
sandwiches 178
avocado
  escalopes of pork with avocado
    and sage 76
Ayrshire bacon 85

B

back fat 215
bacon
  ancient customs 86–87
  Asturian bean stew 95
  bacon, mushroom mostarda
    sandwiches 107
  bacon, roast cherry tomato
    feta sandwiches 107
  bacon around the world 87–91
  bath chaps 85–86
  bigos 201
  BLT 106
  for breakfast 244
  country pâté 205
  cured chine 86
  curing bacon 82–86
  Dean & Deluca croque signor 104
  faggots 241
  frisée and bacon salad 101
  German roast pork 43
  leek and smoked bacon risotto 99
  meat loaf 211
  olla podrida 188

pork and pistachio terrine 206
pounti 192
ragged Jack kale with smoked bacon
  & Anster cheese 97
salad of bitter greens with poached eggs
  & prosciutto 102
smoking bacon 84
spaghetti carbonara 96
steamed pork, bacon & leek pudding 94
traditional cassoulet 250–252
baked chops in foil with apple & honey 75
bamboo shoots
  hot and sour soup 52–53
barding 215, 224–225
basil
  tomato, ham and herb tarts 134
bath chaps 85–86, 234
batvia
  salad of bitter greens with poached
    eggs & prosciutto 102
bay leaves
  Asturian bean stew 95
  bath chaps 234
  bigos 201
  braised belly pork with fennel 59
  brawn 238–239
  Castillian pig's trotters 253
  cheat's cassoulet 249
  choucroute garni 196
  cinghiale in dolce-forte 62–63
  country pâté 205
  feijoada 133
  olla podrida 188
  petit salé 197

pied de cochon Ste Menéhould 254–255
pork and pistachio terrine 206
pork pies 256–257
stock 259
tomato sauce 260
bean curd
hot and sour soup 52–53
beans, black
feijoada 133
beans, white
Asturian bean stew 95
cheat's cassoulet 249
Galician soup 198
tortilla con chorizo 187
beef
meatballs in tomato sauce 191
olla podrida 188
beetroot
sausage, apple & beetroot
sandwiches 179
belly pork 26
boiled pork belly with lentils 60–61
braised belly pork with fennel 59
cheat's cassoulet 249
faggots 241
homemade sausages 174
meat loaf 211
petit salé 197
pounti 192
rillettes 210
steamed pork, bacon & leek pudding 94
big breakfast, the 242–245
bigos 201
black beans
feijoada 133
black puddings 160–169
for breakfast 244
black treacle
American sauce 78
to cook a ham in comfort 126
blade pork 26
blood puddings 160–169
BLT 106
boiled pork belly with lentils 60–61
bouquet garni
pea and ham soup 139
pork pies 256–257
traditional cassoulet 250–252
Bradenham ham 109–110
braised belly pork with fennel 59
brandy
country pâté 205
devilled kidneys 245
pig(eon) terrine 209
pork and pistachio terrine 206
brawn 223, 238–239

Brazilian dishes
feijoada 133
bread
bacon, mushroom & mostarda
sandwiches 107
bacon, roast cherry tomato &
feta sandwiches 107
BLT 106
buttery rowies 242
Dean & Dulca croque signor 104
French toast 245
fricadeller 202
frisée and bacon salad 101
pounti 192
sausage, apple & beetroot
sandwiches 179
sausage, aubergine & courgette
sandwiches 178
sausage, lettuce & rhubarb
sandwiches 178
sausage in brioche 180–181
white bread 265
breadcrumbs
faggots 241
meat loaf 211
meatballs in tomato sauce 191
pied de cochon Ste Menéhould 254–255
Scotch eggs 182
British black puddings 161–163
British ham 109–111
British sausages 146–147
Burmese golden pork 50
buttery rowies 242
buying pork 23

C
cabbage
Galician soup 198
homemade choucroute 195
cakes
lardy cake 264
capers
salsa verde 103
sauce gribiche 262
caraway seeds
choucroute garni 196
Hungarian goulash 64
pork fillet with caraway & tomatoes 57
carrots
boiled pork belly with lentils 60–61
Castillian pig's trotters 253
cheat's cassoulet 249
cinghiale in dolce-forte 62–63
to cook a ham in comfort 126
ham, chicken & mushroom pie 130–131
Madeira sauce 261

olla podrida 188
pea and ham soup 139
stock 259
tomato sauce 260
traditional cassoulet 250–252
casseroles and stews
Asturian bean stew 95
bigos 201
casserole of pork with fresh herbs
& ale 68–69
cheat's cassoulet 249
feijoada 133
olla podrida 188
Spanish stew with tripe &
chickpeas 185
traditional cassoulet 250–252
Castillian pig's trotters 253
caul fat 215
faggots 241
cayenne pepper
American sauce 78
Hungarian goulash 64
celery
American sauce 78
boiled pork belly with lentils 60–61
cinghiale in dolce-forte 62–63
to cook a ham in comfort 126
ham, chicken & mushroom pie 130–131
stock 259
tomato sauce 260
charcuterie, the art of 17–18
cheat's cassoulet 249
cheek 229
bath chaps 234
cheese
bacon, roast cherry tomato & feta
sandwiches 107
Dean & Deluca croque signor 104
leek and ham with cheese sauce 127
leek and smoked bacon risotto 99
meatballs in tomato sauce 191
ragged Jack kale with smoked bacon
& Anster cheese 97
spaghetti carbonara 96
chervil
casserole of pork with fresh herbs
& ale 68–69
chicken
ham, chicken & mushroom pie 130–131
chicken livers
pig(eon) terrine 209
pork and pistachio terrine 206
chickpeas
olla podrida 188
Spanish stew with tripe
& chickpeas 185

chicory
   pork chops with chicory & lemon 67
chilli powder
   Burmese golden pork 50
   cinghiale in dolce-forte 62–63
chillies
   brawn 238–239
   slow-roast shoulder of pork 42
chitterlings 222
chives
   loin of pork with lemon
     & mushroom sauce 73
   pounti 192
chocolate
   cinghiale in dolce-forte 62–63
chops 26
   baked chops in foil with apple
     & honey 75
   choucroute garni 196
   pork chops with chicory and lemon 67
choucroute 194–195
choucroute garni 196
cider
   baked chops in foil with apple
     & honey 75
   meat loaf 211
   ragout of pork with prunes and leeks 66
cinghiale in dolce-forte 62–63
cinnamon
   cinghiale in dolce-forte 62–63
   lardy cake 264
cloves
   to cook a ham in comfort 126
   pied de cochon Ste Menéhould 254–255
   pork and pistachio terrine 206
coriander
   casserole of pork with fresh herbs
     & ale 68–69
   red pepper sauce 78
country pâté 205
courgettes
   sausage, aubergine & courgette
     sandwiches 178
crackling 44
cream
   fricadeller 202
   ham, chicken & mushroom pie 130–131
   ham and haddie 128
   kidneys with mustard
     & mushrooms 236
   loin of pork with mustard
     & vermouth 48–49
   pea and ham soup 139
   pig(eon) terrine 209
   pork and pistachio terrine 206
   pork fillet with caraway & tomatoes 57

pork with creamed leeks 72
   ragout of pork with prunes and leeks 66
cucumbers
   salsa verde 103
cured chine 86
curing bacon 82–86
curing ham 108
curly endive
   frisée and bacon salad 101
cuts
   belly pork 26
   blade pork 26
   buying pork 23
   choosing pork 22
   diced pork 28
   fillet of pork 28
   identifying 24–25
   leg of pork 28–29
   loin of pork 29
   off cuts 223, 226–229
   offal 221–229
   pork fat 214–221
   rack of pork 29
   shoulder of pork 30
   spare ribs 30
   steaks 30
   storing pork 23
   tenderloin of pork 28

D
devilled kidneys 245
diced pork 28
dill
   fricadeller 202
dressings for salads
   shallot vinaigrette 102
   vinaigrette dressing 101
dry-cured bacon 84
duck
   cheat's cassoulet 249

E
ears
   crackling 44
   olla podrida 188
   pork pies 256–257
eggs
   country pâté 205
   faggots 241
   French toast 245
   fricadeller 202
   ham with asparagus & Hollandaise 136
   hot and sour soup 52–53
   meat loaf 211
   meatballs in tomato sauce 191
   pig(eon) terrine 209

pork and leek pie 47
pork and pistachio terrine 206
pork pies 256–257
pounti 192
salad of bitter greens with poached
   eggs & prosciutto 102
salad with potato & mustard
   dressing 103
sauce gribiche 262
sausage in brioche 180–181
Scotch eggs 182
spaghetti carbonara 96
sweet and sour pork 54
tortilla con chorizo 187
elderflower cordial
   roast rolled leg of pork with sesame
     potatoes & wild garlic apple sauce 39
escalopes of pork with avocado & sage 76

F
faggots 241
fat, pork 214–221
feijoada 133
fennel
   braised belly pork with fennel 59
   slow-roast shoulder of pork 42
festivals, black pudding 168–169
fillet of pork 28
   escalopes of pork with avocado
     & sage 76
   medallions of pork with orange 56
   pork fillet with caraway & tomatoes 57
   pork with creamed leeks 72
   pork with plums 70
   ragout of pork with prunes and leeks 66
freezing pork 23
French toast 245
fricadeller 202
frisée and bacon salad 101
fruit
   as an accompaniment to pork 35
   prosciutto with fruits 103
   see also apples; lemons etc.
fruit, dried
   lardy cake 264
     see also prunes; raisins; sultanas

G
Galician soup 198
gammon
   Asturian bean stew 95
   to cook a ham in comfort 126
   pork pies 256–257
ginger
   Burmese golden pork 50
   faggots 241

pied de cochon Ste Menéhould 254–255
sweet and sour pork 54
groundnut oil
  Burmese golden pork 50
  frisée and bacon salad 101
  hot and sour soup 52–53
  medallions of pork with orange 56
  pig(eon) terrine 209
  pork fillet with caraway & tomatoes 57
  pork with creamed leeks 72
  sauce gribiche 262
  Scotch eggs 182
  vinaigrette dressing 101

H
haddock, smoked
  ham and haddie 128
ham
  to cook a ham in comfort 126
  curing 108
  feijoada 133
  Galician soup 198
  ham, chicken & mushroom pie 130–131
  ham and haddie 128
  ham around the world 109–122
  ham with asparagus & Hollandaise 136
  leek and ham with cheese sauce 127
  olla podrida 188
  pea and ham soup 139
  pork and pistachio terrine 206
  pork pies 256–257
  smoking 109
  tomato, ham and herb tarts 134
  understanding the labels 112, 113, 115,
    121
heart 226
  faggots 241
herb-roast pork 225
herbs for pork 35
  see also sage; thyme etc.
hog roast 268–273
Hollandaise sauce 136
homemade mash 176
homemade sausages 174–177
honey
  baked chops in foil with apple
    & honey 75
  bigos 201
  honey pork with roast potatoes
    & apples 40
  pig's liver with lemon and honey 146
  pork with plums 70
  sweet and sour sauce 78
honey pork with roast potatoes
  & apples 40
hot and sour soup 52–53

Hungarian bacon 91
Hungarian goulash 64

I
intensively reared pork 22
Irish bacon 87

J
juniper berries
  bath chaps 234
  bigos 201
  braised belly pork with fennel 59
  choucroute garni 196
  petit salé 197

K
kale
  Galician soup 198
  ragged Jack kale with smoked bacon
    & Anster cheese 97
kidney fat 215
kidneys
  devilled kidneys 245
  kidneys with mustard
    & mushrooms 236
  steamed pork, bacon & leek pudding 94

L
lamb
  traditional cassoulet 250–252
lard 214–221
lardy cake 264
leaf fat 215
leeks
  boiled pork belly with lentils 60–61
  cheat's cassoulet 249
  to cook a ham in comfort 126
  leek and ham with cheese sauce 127
  leek and smoked bacon risotto 99
  pork and leek pie 47
  pork with creamed leeks 72
  ragout of pork with prunes and leeks 66
  steamed pork, bacon & leek pudding 94
leg of pork 28–29
  Burmese golden pork 50
  country pâté 205
  pork and leek pie 47
  roast rolled leg of pork with sesame
    potatoes & wild garlic apple sauce 39
lemons
  braised belly pork with fennel 59
  brawn 238–239
  escalopes of pork with avocado
    & sage 76
  ham with asparagus & Hollandaise 136
  loin of pork with lemon &

mushroom sauce 73
  pig's liver with lemon & honey 146
  pork chops with chicory & lemon 67
  sausage in brioche 180–181
  slow-roast shoulder of pork 42
lentils
  boiled pork belly with lentils 60–61
lettuce
  BLT 106
  sausage, lettuce & rhubarb
    sandwiches 178
liver 222, 226
  faggots 241
  pig's liver with lemon & honey 146
loin of pork 29
  Burmese golden pork 50
  country pâté 205
  German roast pork 43
  honey pork with roast potatoes
    & apples 40
  loin of pork with lemon &
    mushroom sauce 73
  loin of pork with mustard
    & vermouth 48–49
lunch dishes *see* snacks and light lunches

M
mace
  rillettes 210
  Scotch eggs 182
Madeira sauce 261
main courses
  Asturian bean stew 95
  baked chops in foil with apple
    & honey 75
  bath chaps 234
  bigos 201
  boiled pork belly with lentils 60–61
  braised belly pork with fennel 59
  brawn 238–239
  Burmese golden pork 50
  casserole of pork with fresh herbs
    & ale 68–69
  Castillian pig's trotters 253
  cheat's cassoulet 249
  choucroute garni 196
  cinghiale in dolce-forte 62–63
  to cook a ham in comfort 126
  escalopes of pork with avocado
    & sage 76
  faggots 241
  feijoada 133
  fricadeller 202
  frisée and bacon salad 101
  German roast pork 43
  ham, chicken & mushroom pie 130–131

herb-roast pork 225
honey pork with roast potatoes
    & apples 40
Hungarian goulash 64
leek and smoked bacon risotto 99
loin of pork with lemon &
    mushroom sauce 73
loin of pork with mustard
    & vermouth 48–49
meat loaf 211
meatballs in tomato sauce 191
medallions of pork with orange 56
olla podrida 188
pease pudding 137
pied de cochon Ste Menéhould 254–255
pig's liver with lemon and honey 146
pork and leek pie 47
pork chops with chicory and lemon 67
pork fillet with caraway & tomatoes 57
pork pies 256–257
pork with creamed leeks 72
pork with plums 70
pounti 192
ragged Jack kale with smoked bacon
    & Anster cheese 97
ragout of pork with prunes and leeks 66
roast rolled leg of pork with sesame
    potatoes & wild garlic apple sauce 39
salad of bitter greens with poached eggs
    and prosciutto 102
salad with potato & mustard
    dressing 103
salsa verde 103
slow-roast shoulder of pork 42
spaghetti carbonara 96
Spanish stew with tripe
    & chickpeas 185
spare ribs 77
steamed pork, bacon & leek pudding 94
sweet and sour pork 54
traditional cassoulet 250–252
marjoram
    baked chops in foil with apple
        & honey 75
    faggots 241
    pied de cochon Ste Menéhould 254–255
    pork pies 256–257
mayonnaise
    BLT 106
meat loaf 211
meatballs in tomato sauce 191
medallions of pork with orange 56
Melton Mowbray pork pies 231
milk
    French toast 245
    fricadeller 202

ham, chicken & mushroom pie 130–131
leek and ham with cheese sauce 127
loin of pork with lemon
    & mushroom sauce 73
pounti 192
sausage in brioche 180–181
mint
    pease pudding 137
mushrooms
    bacon, mushroom & mostarda
        sandwiches 107
    bigos 201
    ham, chicken & mushroom pie 130–131
    hot and sour soup 52–53
    kidneys with mustard
        & mushrooms 236
    loin of pork with lemon
        & mushroom sauce 73
    pork fillet with caraway & tomatoes 57
mustard
    American sauce 78
    devilled kidneys 245
    frisée and bacon salad 101
    honey pork with roast potatoes
        & apples 40
    kidneys with mustard
        & mushrooms 236
    leek and ham with cheese sauce 127
    loin of pork with mustard
        & vermouth 48–49
    meat loaf 211
    medallions of pork with orange 56
    pork and leek pie 47
    salad with potato & mustard
        dressing 103
    sauce gribiche 262
    sausage, lettuce & rhubarb
        sandwiches 178
    shallot vinaigrette 102
    sweet and sour sauce 78
    vinaigrette dressing 101

N
nutmeg
    cinghiale in dolce-forte 62–63
    faggots 241
    lardy cake 264
    pork & pistachio terrine 206
    rillettes 210
nuts
    Castillian pig's trotters 253
    pork and pistachio terrine 206

O
oatmeal
    skirlie 263

offal 221–229
    see also kidneys; liver etc.
olla podrida 188
one-pot dishes
    Asturian bean stew 95
    bigos 201
    cheat's cassoulet 249
    feijoada 133
    honey pork with roast potatoes
        & apples 40
    Hungarian goulash 64
    olla podrida 188
    Spanish stew with tripe &
        chickpeas 185
    traditional cassoulet 250–252
onions
    American sauce 78
    Asturian bean stew 95
    bigos 201
    boiled pork belly with lentils 60–61
    Burmese golden pork 50
    casserole of pork with fresh herbs
        & ale 68–69
    Castillian pig's trotters 253
    cheat's cassoulet 249
    choucroute garni 196
    cinghiale in dolce-forte 62–63
    to cook a ham in comfort 126
    country pâté 205
    devilled kidneys 245
    faggots 241
    fricadeller 202
    ham, chicken & mushroom pie 130–131
    honey pork with roast potatoes
        & apples 40
    Hungarian goulash 64
    kidneys with mustard
        & mushrooms 236
    meat loaf 211
    meatballs in tomato sauce 191
    olla podrida 188
    pork and leek pie 47
    pork and pistachio terrine 206
    pork pies 256–257
    pounti 192
    skirlie 263
    Spanish stew with tripe
        & chickpeas 185
    stock 259
    sweet and sour pork 54
    tomato sauce 260
    traditional cassoulet 250–252
orange juice
    medallions of pork with orange 56
oranges
    cinghiale in dolce-forte 62–63

feijoada 133
medallions of pork with orange 56
tomato sauce 260
oregano
Dean & Deluca croque signor 104
organic pork 22

P
paprika
American sauce 78
Asturian bean stew 95
Castillian pig's trotters 253
Galician soup 198
Hungarian goulash 64
Spanish stew with tripe
& chickpeas 185
Parma ham 117
parsley
boiled pork belly with lentils 60–61
brawn 238–239
casserole of pork with fresh herbs
& ale 68–69
to cook a ham in comfort 126
devilled kidneys 245
ham, chicken & mushroom pie 130–131
loin of pork with mustard
& vermouth 48–49
meatballs in tomato sauce 191
medallions of pork with orange 56
olla podrida 188
pork and leek pie 47
pork pies 256–257
pounti 192
sauce gribiche 262
stock 259
pasta
spaghetti carbonara 96
pastis
braised belly pork with fennel 59
pastry, making 263
pastry dishes
ham, chicken & mushroom pie 130–131
pork and leek pie 47
pork pies 230–231, 256–257
sausage rolls 184
tomato, ham and herb tarts 134
pâtés
country pâté 205
peas
pea and ham soup 139
pease pudding 137
peppercorns
bath chaps 234
boiled pork belly with lentils 60–61
brawn 238–239
to cook a ham in comfort 126

petit salé 197
pork and leek pie 47
peppers, red
Hungarian goulash 64
red pepper sauce 78
sweet and sour pork 54
petit salé 197
pied de cochon Ste Menéhould 254–255
pies
ham, chicken & mushroom pie 130–131
making pastry 263
pork and leek pie 47
pork pies 230–231, 256–257
pig ears
for crackling 44
olla podrida 188
pig(eon) terrine 209
pig's liver with lemon and honey 146
pine nuts
cinghiale in dolce-forte 62–63
pistachio nuts
pork and pistachio terrine 206
plums
pork with plums 70
Polish dishes
bigos 201
Polony 147
pork and leek pie 47
pork and pistachio terrine 206
pork chops with chicory and lemon 67
pork fat 214–221
pork fillet with caraway and tomatoes 57
pork pies 230–231, 256–257
pork scratchings 216, 258
pork with creamed leeks 72
pork with plums 70
Portuguese blood puddings 165
Portuguese hog roast 270
Portuguese sausages 158
potatoes
Galician soup 198
homemade mash 176
honey pork with roast potatoes
& apples 40
Hungarian goulash 64
pea and ham soup 139
roast rolled leg of pork with sesame
potatoes & wild garlic apple sauce 39
salad with potato & mustard
dressing 103
poultry see chicken; duck
pounti 192
prosciutto with fruits 103
prunes
bigos 201
pounti 192

ragout of pork with prunes and leeks 66
puddings
pease pudding 137
steamed pork, bacon & leek pudding 94
Puy lentils
boiled pork belly with lentils 60–61

R
rack of pork 29
radicchio
salad of bitter greens with poached
eggs & prosciutto 102
ragged Jack kale with smoked bacon
& Anster cheese 97
ragout of pork with prunes and leeks 66
raisins
cinghiale in dolce-forte 62–63
rapeseed oil
salad with potato & mustard
dressing 103
red pepper sauce 78
red peppers
Hungarian goulash 64
red pepper sauce 78
sweet and sour pork 54
red wine
cinghiale in dolce-forte 62–63
rendering the fat 215–216
rhubarb
sausage, lettuce & rhubarb
sandwiches 178
ribs 30, 77
feijoada 133
olla podrida 188
sauces for 78
rice
leek and smoked bacon risotto 99
rice wine
sweet and sour pork 54
rillettes 210
risotto
leek and smoked bacon risotto 99
roast pork
German roast pork 43
herb-roast pork 225
honey pork with roast potatoes
& apples 40
roast rolled leg of pork with sesame
potatoes & wild garlic apple sauce 39
slow-roast shoulder of pork 42
rosemary
braised belly pork with fennel 59
pork with plums 70
rillettes 210

S

saffron
　Asturian bean stew 95
sage
　boiled pork belly with lentils 60–61
　brawn 238–239
　escalopes of pork with avocado
　　& sage 76
　faggots 241
　honey pork with roast potatoes
　　& apples 40
　meat loaf 211
　pork pies 256–257
　steamed pork, bacon & leek pudding 94
salads 100
　frisée and bacon salad 101
　salad of bitter greens with poached
　　eggs & prosciutto 102
　salad with potato & mustard
　　dressing 103
　salsa verde 103
salami 155–157
salsa verde 103
salt, for curing bacon 84
sandwiches
　bacon, roast cherry tomato & feta
　　sandwiches 106
　BLT 106
　sausage, apple & beetroot
　　sandwiches 179
　sausage, aubergine & courgette
　　sandwiches 178
　sausage, lettuce & rhubarb
　　sandwiches 178
sauces
　American sauce 78
　dill sauce 202
　Hollandaise sauce 136
　Madeira sauce 261
　red pepper sauce 78
　sauce gribiche 262
　sweet and sour sauce 78
　tomato sauce 260
sauerkraut 35, 194–195
　bigos 201
　choucroute garni 196
sausage rolls 184
sausagemeat
　sausage rolls 184
　Scotch eggs 182
sausages 144–145
　Asturian bean stew 95
　bigos 201
　for breakfast 244
　cheat's cassoulet 249
　choucroute garni 196

feijoada 133
Galician soup 198
making sausages 172–177
olla podrida 188
pea and ham soup 139
sausage in brioche 180–181
sausage sandwiches 178–179
sausages around the world 146–158
Spanish stew with tripe &
　chickpeas 185
tortilla con chorizo 187
traditional cassoulet 250–252
saveloys 147
Scotch eggs 182
Scottish black puddings 161–163
Scottish dishes
　buttery rowies 242
　pork with creamed leeks 72
　ragged Jack kale with smoked bacon
　　& Anster cheese 97
seafood, and pork 35
sesame oil
　Burmese golden pork 50
　hot and sour soup 52–53
sesame seeds
　roast rolled leg of pork with sesame
　　potatoes & wild garlic apple sauce 39
shallots
　honey pork with roast potatoes
　　& apples 40
　Madeira sauce 261
　salsa verde 103
　shallot vinaigrette 102
sherry
　steamed pork, bacon & leek pudding 94
　sweet and sour pork 54
shoulder of pork 30
　Hungarian goulash 64
　pork pies 256–257
　slow-roast shoulder of pork 42
　traditional cassoulet 250–252
side dishes
　sauerkraut 35, 194–195
　skirlie 263
skirlie 263
slaughtering pigs 16–17
slow-roast shoulder of pork 42
smoking bacon 84
smoking ham 109
snacks and light lunches
　bacon, mushroom & mostarda
　　sandwiches 107
　bacon, roast cherry tomato & feta
　　sandwiches 107
　BLT 106
　country pâté 205

Dean & Deluca croque signor 104
Galician soup 198
ham and haddie 128
ham with asparagus & Hollandaise 136
leek and ham with cheese sauce 127
pea and ham soup 139
pig(eon) terrine 209
pork and pistachio terrine 206
pork pies 256–257
rillettes 210
sausage, apple & beetroot
　sandwiches 179
sausage, aubergine & courgette
　sandwiches 178
sausage, lettuce & rhubarb
　sandwiches 178
sausage in brioche 180–181
sausage rolls 184
Scotch eggs 182
tortilla con chorizo 187
soups
　Galician soup 198
　hot and sour soup 52–53
　pea and ham soup 139
soy sauce
　hot and sour soup 52–53
　red pepper sauce 78
　sweet and sour pork 54
　sweet and sour sauce 78
spaghetti carbonara 96
spare ribs 30, 77
　olla podrida 188
spices for pork 35
　see also cinnamon; ginger etc.
spicy sage sausage mix 177
spleen 226
starters
　frisée and bacon salad 101
　Galician soup 198
　ham with asparagus & Hollandaise 136
　hot and sour soup 52–53
　pea and ham soup 139
　prosciutto with fruits 103
　ragged Jack kale with smoked bacon
　　and Anster cheese 97
　salad of bitter greens with poached
　　eggs & prosciutto 102
　salad with potato and mustard
　　dressing 103
　salsa verde 103
　tomato, ham & herb tarts 134
steaks 30
steamed pork, bacon & leek pudding 94
stock, making 259
storing pork 23
suet

steamed pork, bacon & leek pudding 94
Suffolk ham 111
Suffolk sweet-cured bacon 85
sultanas
    pig(eon) terrine 209
supper dishes
    ham and haddie 128
    ham with asparagus & Hollandaise 136
    kidneys with mustard
        & mushrooms 236
    leek and ham with cheese sauce 127
    rillettes 210
Swedish dishes
    fricadeller 202
sweet and sour pork 54
sweet and sour sauce 78
sweet-cured bacon 84
sweetbreads 222

T
tails
    pork pies 256–257
tarragon
    casserole of pork with fresh herbs
        & ale 68–69
    sauce gribiche 262
tarts
    tomato, ham and herb tarts 134
tenderloin of pork 28
terrines
    pig(eon) terrine 209
    pork and pistachio terrine 206
thyme
    cinghiale in dolce-forte 62–63
    to cook a ham in comfort 126
    country pâté 205
    faggots 241
    petit salé 197
    pork and leek pie 47
    ragout of pork with prunes and leeks 66
    rillettes 210
    stock 259
    tomato, ham and herb tarts 134
    tomato sauce 260
tiger lily buds, dried
    hot and sour soup 52–53
to cook a ham in comfort 126
tomato, ham and herb tarts 134
tomato purée
    American sauce 78
    bigos 201
    cheat's cassoulet 249
    Madeira sauce 261
    sweet and sour pork 54
    sweet and sour sauce 78
    traditional cassoulet 250–252

tomato sauce 260
tomatoes
    bacon, roast cherry tomato & feta
        sandwiches 107
    BLT 106
    braised belly pork with fennel 59
    cheat's cassoulet 249
    Hungarian goulash 64
    pork fillet with caraway & tomatoes 57
    red pepper sauce 78
    Spanish stew with tripe
        & chickpeas 185
    tomato, ham and herb tarts 134
    tomato sauce 260
    traditional cassoulet 250–252
tongue 222
tortilla con chorizo 187
traditional cassoulet 250–252
tripe
    Spanish stew with tripe
        & chickpeas 185
trotters 226, 229
    Castillian pig's trotters 253
    feijoada 133
    olla podrida 188
    pied de cochon Ste Menéhould 254–255
    pork pies 256–257
    traditional cassoulet 250–252
turmeric
    Burmese golden pork 50
turnips
    Galician soup 198
    olla podrida 188

V
veal
    country pâté 205
    pork pies 256–257
vegetables see carrots; leeks etc.
vermouth
    loin of pork with mustard & vermouth
        48–49
    medallions of pork with orange 56
vinaigrettes
    shallot vinaigrette 102
    vinaigrette dressing 101

W
wet-cured bacon 84
white beans
    Asturian bean stew 95
    cheat's cassoulet 249
    Galician soup 198
    tortilla con chorizo 187
white bread 265
white wine

braised belly pork with fennel 59
Castillian pig's trotters 253
choucroute garni 196
ham with asparagus & Hollandaise 136
leek and smoked bacon risotto 99
medallions of pork with orange 56
pied de cochon Ste Menéhould 254–255
pork chops with chicory and lemon 67
pork with creamed leeks 72
Spanish stew with tripe
    & chickpeas 185
traditional cassoulet 250–252
wild boar 32–33
    cinghiale in dolce-forte 62–63
Wiltshire sausage mix 177
wine see red wine; rice wine; white wine
Worcestershire sauce
    American sauce 78

Y
yeast
    buttery rowies 242
    sausage in brioche 180–181
    white bread 265
York ham 111

bibliography

BIANCHI, Anne, *Italian Festival Food*. John Wiley and Sons, 1999.

BREARS, Peter, *Cooking and Dining in Medieval England*. Prospect Books, 2008.

DAVIDSON, Alan, *The Oxford Companion to Food*. Oxford University Press, 2006.

FISHER, M.F.K, *The Art of Eating*. Random House, 1988.

GARAVINI, Daniela, *Pigs and Pork*. Konnemann, 1999.

HARTLEY, Dorothy, *Food in England*. Piatkus Books, 2009.

HUTCHINS, Sheila, *English Recipes*. Methuen, 1967.

LUARD, Elisabeth, *European Peasant Cookery*. Grub Street, 2007.

MASON, Laura and Brown, Catherine, *The Taste of Britain*. HarperPress, 2006.

METZGER, Christine, *Culinaria Germany*. Ullman, 2008.

MONTAGNE, Prosper, *Larousse Gastronomique*. Hamlyn, 2001.

PIRAS, Claudia, *Culinaria Italy*. Ullman, 2008.

QUALE, Eric, *Old Cook Books*. Studio Vista, 1978.

ROSENGARTEN, David (with Joel Dean and Giorgio Deluca), *The Dean and Deluca Cookbook*. Random House, 1996.

TRUTTER, Marian, *Culinaria Spain*. Konnemann, 2004.

ULLMAN, H. F., *Culinaria France*. Ullman, 2008.

WATSON, Lyall, *The Whole Hog*. Profile Books Ltd, 2004.

Food Writer Heros

Nigel Slater

Sybil Kapoor

Fergus Henderson

The River café ladies especially in memory of Rose Gray

Simon Hopkinson

Anthony Demetre

acknowledgements

Christopher Trotter

Thanks to Anova Books and Katie Deane for making my idea become a reality and Georgie for the wonderful design. To Carol Wilson, may we write many more books together, to my family for support and patience with constant pork on the menu. Tom Mitchell Pig farmer extraordinaire. Bruce Bennett at Pillars of Hercules for employing interesting colleagues who gave me ideas. Jenny White from Myres castle for allowing me time to 'play' with the pigs. David Naylor for the many conversations on pig practicalities and recipe perceptions. Maggie the recipe tester and most of all to the great beasts themselves – the pig the most civilised and intelligent of animals, may we ensure that the pigs we eat have had a happy life.

Carol Wilson

The many butchers, pig farmers and food producers who helped with much useful information, in particular:

Andrew Holt of The Real Lancashire Black Pudding Company

Emmett's of Peasenhall

Melton Mowbray Pie Association.

The idea stemmed from discussions with Christopher Trotter's
father-in-law Richard Bilton – to whose memory this book
is dedicated – who also loved pigs and cured his own hams
& made sausages.

First published in Great Britain in 2010 by
Pavilion Books
Old West London Magistrates Court
10 Southcombe Street
London, W14 0RA

An imprint of the Anova Books Company Ltd

Picture credits
pg 10: ©The Art Archive/Alamy
pg 14-15: ©Tim Pannell/Corbis
pg 88-89: ©imagebroker/Alamy

Publisher: Anna Cheifetz
Designer: Georgina Hewitt
Project editor: Katie Deane
Copy editor: Barbara Dixon
Proofreader: Caroline Curtis
Recipe rester: Maggie Ramsay
Indexer: Sandra Shotter
Photography: Diana Miller
Stylist: Wei Tang
Illustrator: Murdo Culver

ISBN 978-1-86205-861-3

A CIP catalogue record for this book is available from
the British Library.

10 9 8 7 6 5 4 3 2 1

Reproduction by Dot Gradations Ltd, UK
Printed and bound in China by 1010 Printing
International Limited

www.anovabooks.com